This item is due for return on or before the last date below.
It may be renewed by telephone, in person or via the Internet at
http://ipac.northlan.gov.uk if not required by another borrower.

SHANKLY

FROM GLENBUCK TO WEMBLEY

PHIL THOMPSON & STEVE HALE

TEMPUS

First published 2004

Tempus Publishing Limited
The Mill, Brimscombe Port,
Stroud, Gloucestershire, GL5 2QG
www.tempus-publishing.com

British Library Cataloguing in Publication Data.
A catalogue record for this book is available from the British Library.

ISBN 0 7524 2943 4

Typesetting and origination by Tempus Publishing Limited
Printed and bound in Great Britain

CONTENTS

1

THE BOY FROM GLENBUCK

Bill Shankly was born on 2 September 1913, in the coal-mining village of Glenbuck, Ayrshire. At the time of his birth, the population of Glenbuck was declining and totalled about 600 people. This was a time when it was becoming increasingly difficult to obtain good quality coal from the local mines and it led to a gradual exoduss from Glenbuck to the nearby villages, where a better quality of coal and prospects of more stable employment were available. On leaving school at the age of fourteen, it was inevitable that Bill would begin work at the nearby pit and it was an experience that would affect him deeply. His first job at the pit was sorting out the coal from the stones and then returning the empty truck back down the pit. He would earn extra money on a Sunday emptying coal wagons with a shovel at a rate of sixpence a ton. All of this work took place at the pit top but, within six months, he was sent to work at the pit bottom. Here, for the first time, he experienced the full horror of what it was like to work as a miner during the days before nationalization drastically improved their lot. Health and safety were at a premium and the stench of damp, lack of ventilation and atrocious conditions that the miner had to work in were never forgotten by Shankly. Although he did acknowledge that conditions improved for them during the post-war years, he knew the struggle that the miners had to go through to achieve better

Glenbuck, c. 1910.

working conditions and throughout his life he had great sympathy
with their plight.

After a two-year period working underground, the pit was closed
and Shankly was made redundant. For the first time in his life,
Shankly had to sign on the dole. With the prospect of employment
in Glenbuck and its nearby areas virtually non-existent, Shankly
spent his time walking or, if he had any spare money, playing cards.
He even helped his sister Elizabeth with her paper round.

Bill was the youngest in a family of five boys and five girls. As was
the case with the majority of working-class boys in Britain during
this period, football was an obsession in the village. It can be said
that football was in the blood of the Shankly family with Bill's
mother, Barbara, having two brothers who were professional foot-
ballers. Bob Blyth played for Rangers, Middlesbrough, Preston
North End, Dundee and Portsmouth and Bill Blyth played for
Preston North End and Carlisle United. It was no surprise,
therefore, that as soon as they were old enough to kick a ball, the
Shankly boys came under the spell of football and practised and
played the game constantly. The fact that all five of them were to
become professional footballers was an incredible achievement. Alec,

the oldest boy, was the first to sign professional terms and played for Ayr United and Clyde. The rest of the Shankly boys followed suit with James playing for Portsmouth, Halifax Town, Coventry City, Carlisle United, Sheffield United, Southend United and Barrow; John playing for Portsmouth, Luton Town, Blackpool, Alloa and Morton; Bob playing for Alloa, Tunbridge Wells and Falkirk; and finally Bill, who played for Carlisle United and Preston North End.

Sporting prowess was not restricted to Barbara's side of the family, however. Bill's father, John, who worked originally as a postman and then as a bespoke tailor, was a quarter-mile runner of some note. John Shankly played football only during his school days but always maintained a high level of fitness.

Life was not easy for Barbara and John Shankly and bringing up their five sons and five daughters (Netta, Elizabeth, Isobel, Barbara and Jean) on very little money was later described by Bill as a miracle. Like his son, John did not smoke or drink but loved to go to the cinema. It was an eight-mile round trip to the nearest one but John would often make the journey on foot to watch a movie. John Shankly was known as an honest, straight-talking man. Barbara was a woman who, though she had little, would share what she had with anyone. It was these characteristics of his parents that were ingrained in Bill and helped to mould a man who would be idolised by many thousands, as much for the warmth and uniqueness of his personality as for his incredible ability as a football manager.

Shankly was offered a trial with his famous village team, Glenbuck Cherrypickers, but was considered too young at sixteen to join them. Within a year, the Cherrypickers had folded and Shankly never had the chance to represent his village. Shankly began to display his notable football prowess after this with local junior team Cronberry. It was here that he learned how to look after himself, playing with and against men many years his senior. He was always keen to point out that although it was called junior football it was junior in name only: there was no age limit and he would often come up against experienced men who played the game hard. It was also while at Cronberry that a scout recommended him to

Bill Blyth, a director at Carlisle United and, of course, Shankly's uncle, who was a key figure in the development of the all-action half-back. Shankly was invited to Brunton Park for trials.

On his first trip out of Scotland, Bill, seventeen at the time, was accompanied to Carlisle by his brother Alec. After his trial match, on 20 August and just one game, a reserve match against Middlesbrough Reserves on 27 August 1932 which Carlisle lost 6-0, Shankly had shown enough promise to warrant an offer of professional terms with Carlisle. He was initially on a month's trial but was soon signed up for the rest of the season and, thankfully, his brief taste of unemployment was at an end. Guided by trainer Tommy Curry and team manager Tom Hampson, Shankly forced himself into the first team. Becoming a professional allowed Shankly to train even harder; his objective being that one should be fit enough to play flat out for not ninety minutes but 120 minutes.

Shankly played regularly for the reserves through the rest of 1932 and, on 31 December, made his full league debut for Carlisle against Rochdale, which ended in a 2-2 draw. He played 16 games over the rest of the season, all at right half and by April a local newspaper commented that 'Shankly is a most promising player. He is attracting attention!' At the end of the 1932/33 season, Carlisle finished in 19th place and many of the team received free transfers. Shankly, however, was offered and signed a new contract.

After a happy season learning his trade at Carlisle, Shankly travelled home to Glenbuck content with life and looking forward to the summer break. He was by now a first-team regular and was being paid a weekly wage of £4 10s to play a game that he would gladly have played for nothing. When he compared his occupation with that of the miner, he knew he was well off. Shankly later recalled his thoughts at the time: *'For as long as I can remember my sole aim in life was to play football. When I worked down the pit in Scotland, all I dreamed about was the end of the shift and legging it to the nearest field for a game.'*

Shankly's close-season break was brought to an abrupt end when a telegram arrived at his family home from Carlisle United. It instructed him to report back to Brunton Park the following day but gave no other hint of what he was being summoned back to Carlisle for. Once again, Alec accompanied his younger brother and, on their arrival at Carlisle, Shankly's Uncle Bill informed him that a Preston North End representative, Bill Scott, was waiting to speak to him. Before introducing Scott, Blyth revealed that Preston had made a £500 offer to Carlisle for Bill Shankly's services for the coming season. They were also willing to offer a personal payment of £60 and wage of £5 a week. At first Shankly turned the offer down: he was happy at Carlisle and the wages Preston were offering were little more than he was already receiving. A disappointed Bill Scott trooped out of Brunton Park, unhappy that he had failed to lure the young Scottish player to the Lancashire club. As soon as Scott had left the room, Alec got to work on Bill, explaining that Preston were once a great team and were capable to becoming so again. It was an opportunity that should be taken. Convinced by Alec's powers of reasoning, the two brothers set off to catch up with Scott, who had by this time departed Carlisle to catch the Newcastle train. They caught up with him just as he was boarding the train and quickly jumped on as it pulled out of the station. Bill explained to a delighted Scott that he would be pleased to join Preston North End and, after signing the appropriate forms, the Shankly brothers alighted the train at the next station and returned to Carlisle. For £500, Preston had captured a player who would give them loyal service for the next sixteen years.

Shankly's last appearance for Carlisle was at home for the reserves against Wallsend on 5 May 1933; a match which, incidentally, ended in a 6-0 win for Carlisle. On hearing news of the sale of Shankly to Preston, Carlisle United's supporters were up in arms but their protests were to no avail and, in July 1933, Shankly reported for pre-season training at Deepdale for the first time. Reports in the Preston newspapers of North End's capture of the promising teenage half-back were low key. There was little hint that they had, in fact, signed a player whom they would soon be describing as a 'human dynamo' and 'an iron man'.

Shankly began his Preston career with a debut for the reserve team in the Central League against Blackpool Reserves. He started with a victory and within a few months had been promoted to the first team. His first-team debut was against Hull City and Preston ran out comfortable 5-0 winners.

Shankly's first season at Deepdale was a momentous one, with Preston regaining a place in the First Division as runners-up to Second Division Champions Grimsby Town. Preston North End's football correspondent at the time, Walter Pilkington, was clearly impressed with Shankly's first season at the club and in his end of season notes he wrote: *'One of this season's discoveries, Bill Shankly, played with rare tenacity and uncommonly good ideas for a lad of twenty. He is full of good football and possessed with unlimited energy; he should go far.'* Pilkington also revealed a conversation with Shankly that displayed the ambitions of the young Scot. He recalled: *'I was returning by train from a match at Plymouth in a 'sleeper', with Bill Shankly and Jimmy Dougal as bunk companions. I asked Bill what he wanted most. 'To play for Scotland, sir' he replied, without a moment's hesitation.'*

As with football management, it took Shankly a few years to achieve his objective but his international ambitions were finally realised when he was selected to represent Scotland against England at Wembley, in 1938. Before achieving international honours, however, Shankly had the task of helping Preston consolidate their hard won position back in the First Division. This was achieved with the minimum of fuss and, by the late 1930s, Preston had developed a team that were capable of holding their own against the best in the land. In 1937 Shankly achieved what had been a dream since his days kicking a ball around the village football pitch in Glenbuck: to play in an FA Cup final at Wembley. After victories against Newcastle, Stoke, Exeter, Tottenham Hotspur and West Bromwich Albion, Preston were through to their first cup final since losing to Huddersfield Town in the 1922 final, held at Stamford Bridge. They had won through to Wembley with a goal aggregate of 19 for and 6 against and their form leading up to the final appeared to give them the edge over their opponents, Sunderland. The fact that it had taken Sunderland a total of eight hard-fought matches to get to Wembley was another factor in Preston's favour and they stepped out at Wembley in confident mood.

As the two teams lined up to face each other on May Day 1937, they became the first players to participate in a May cup final. Prior to this date, the FA Cup final was traditionally played on the last Saturday in April. As part of the celebrations to mark the coronation of King George VI, however, the Football Association decided to move the final to the first Saturday in May. King George and Queen Elizabeth were both present on what was a perfect, early summer's day.

It was Preston who were looking the most dangerous from the start. Prompted by half-backs Shankly and Milne (father of future Preston, Liverpool and England star Gordon Milne) Preston kept up the pressure on Sunderland and it was no surprise when F. O'Donnell latched on to a pass from Dougal and blasted the ball past Mapson in the Sunderland goal. In twelve of the previous finals, the team that had scored first at Wembley had gone on to win the Cup and Preston were confident it was to be their day.

If the first half had been all Preston, the second saw a dramatic turnaround, with Sunderland taking total control of the game. Gurney scored an equaliser and Raich Carter, who even then was acknowledged as one of the all-time greats, scored a breathtaking goal to put them into the lead. With nineteen minutes left, Carter glided past full-back Gallimore before slotting the ball past Preston 'keeper Burns. Sunderland's fantastic comeback was completed six minutes later when a sweeping move involving Gurney, Gallagher and Burbanks resulted in Burbanks sealing Preston's fate with a fine finish past the bemused Preston goalkeeper. In later years, Shankly admitted that they were beaten by a far superior team on the day. In many ways the Sunderland team of 1937 played the same brand of 'total football' as the great Holland team of the 1970s, with full-backs Gorman and Hall leading many of their attacks that developed from every section of the team. Shankly once stated that it was a frightening experience to visit Roker Park during the late 1930s because Sunderland were such a terrific outfit.

The following season, 1937/38, was also memorable in many ways for Shankly and his Preston team. He won his much-coveted first Scottish cap and scored his first league goal, on 2 February 1938, against Liverpool. Preston were narrowly pipped in a close race for the League Championship and Shankly returned to Wembley to help his team defeat Huddersfield Town 1-0 in another eventful final.

It was a joyous day for Shankly and his family back home in Glenbuck when news came through that he had been selected to make his international debut on 9 April 1938 against the old enemy, England, at Wembley. Preston, in fact, had four of their players in the Scotland team that day: Bill Shankly, Andy Beattie, Tom Smith and George Mutch. The impact of the Scottish players on the Preston teams of the late 1930s can be gauged from the fact that their 1936 line-up included no less than nine Scots: Shankly, Milone, Beattie, Dougal, Maxwell, Smith, Fagan, F. O'Donnell and H. O'Donnell. It was little wonder that they were known at the time as the 'Preston Scottish'. The call up of Shankly to the Scotland team began a succession of half-backs who would represent their country with an infectious spirit and passion. After Shankly came Scoular, Evans, Docherty and Mackay. All were great half-backs who had a touch of steel about their play.

The England team that took the field against Scotland was quite a formidable line-up and within minutes of the start of the match, Shankly was welcomed to international football by a tackle from England's Wilf Copping that ripped through his shin guard, causing an ugly gash on his leg. The older Copping was determined to make his mark on Shankly as early as possible and this he did, literally! Never one to complain, Shankly played on and helped the Scots to a 1-0 victory, the winning goal being scored by Hearts player Tommy Walker. Arsenal's hard man Copping once again inflicted a painful injury on Shankly during a league game later in Shankly's career. In his autobiography, Shankly admitted he was sad when he heard of Copping's retirement from football, for he had been biding his time waiting for the opportunity to return the compliment.

Two weeks after his international debut, Shankly was back at Wembley to face Huddersfield in the 1938 FA Cup final. Although the match was not a classic, the events of the last minute of the game resulted in it being a cup final that is argued over to this day. Once again Preston were installed as favourites by the bookies and were confidently expected to be too strong for their Yorkshire opponents. Preston had been strongly fancied to land the League Championship all season and it was only at the death that Arsenal took the title, with Wolves runners-up and Preston finishing a close third. In contrast, Huddersfield had been struggling in the lower reaches of the table and had finished in nineteenth position.

The first ninety minutes of the game, the first ever to be broadcast live in its entirety with an estimated 10,000 television viewers following the play, failed to produce a goal. For the first time ever, extra time was played at Wembley and, prompted by the tireless Shankly, Preston were looking the most likely to break the deadlock. With the game entering the last minute of extra time, Shankly fed the ball through to George Mutch. The Preston danger man began to move menacingly towards the Huddersfield penalty area. Alf Young, the Huddersfield centre half and captain, who until this moment had been having an inspired game in the Town defence, thrust out a leg in a desperate attempt to stop Mutch. The Preston forward tumbled to the ground and the referee, Jimmy Jewell, judging the challenge illegal, pointed to the spot. After failing to entice any of his teammates, including the normally ice-cool Shankly, to take on the responsibility of deciding the fate of the FA Cup, Mutch brushed himself down before stepping up to take the penalty that would decide the match. A hush came over Wembley as Mutch ran up and blasted the ball with as much power as he could muster. The shot crashed against the bar before rolling over the line and into the net, leaving the disconsolate Huddersfield 'keeper, Hesford, sprawling helplessly on the lush turf. The Preston supporters erupted as Mutch was mobbed by his teammates, delirious in the knowledge that the cup was returning to Preston for the first time in the century. Alf Young, the man who had conceded the penalty, was in tears as the final whistle blew. As his teammates consoled the sad and dejected figure, the Preston captain Tom Smith strode up to the Royal Box to collect the cup from King George. To this day Huddersfield supporters maintain that photographic evidence suggests that the foul was committed outside the penalty area but, nonetheless, history books tell us that a George Mutch penalty won the FA Cup for Preston in 1938 and the match ball still has the white paint on it from its contact with the newly painted crossbar.

To be part of an FA Cup-winning team at Wembley was always considered by Shankly to be the biggest thrill of his football career. When asked later about the penalty incident, he expressed no doubts.

2

THE WAR YEARS

The outbreak of war in 1939 saw Bill Shankly enlist in the RAF. He approached the services as he approached his life, doing everything he was asked to the best of his ability. He was careful to maintain his high level of fitness and would run the lanes and countryside of wherever he was posted. After being stationed at Padgate and then St Athan, in South Wales, he was sent to a camp in Manchester. Manchester suited Shankly perfectly with regular football and boxing available. While there, he played soccer in the Manchester and District League and won a cup boxing for his camp at middleweight. He was also selected for his second wartime international, being picked to play against England.

When the news came through that he was being posted to Arbroath for a junior NCO's course, Shankly was very disappointed. He had enjoyed his stay at Manchester to such an extent and made friends with so many people that he did not want to leave. After a further posting to Great Yarmouth and then Henlow in Bedfordshire, Shankly was finally stationed in Glasgow for the duration of the war.

While stationed at the various camps, Shankly took every opportunity to guest for the local league clubs, who always seemed to get word of when an international player was stationed nearby. Many servicemen, including Shankly, would risk 'jankers' to turn out when there was no weekend pass for them. Shankly played three games under the name of Newman for Norwich in January 1943. In the first of these, against an Army XI, he scored twice in an 8-4 win for the home team, with the attendance recorded as 484. Whenever possible, clubs protected players who were chancing getting caught for being absent without leave. Team line-ups would not be released until a week or two after the match had taken place. Apart from helping players to keep up a decent standard of match fitness, the small amount of extra cash that the players received in match fees and expenses was a valuable addition to their service pay. An example of the amount that players received can be gauged from Shankly's 30 shilling (£1.50) fee that he received from Cardiff City after playing for them against Lovells Athletic in 1942. Apart from Norwich, Shankly played for Preston, Liverpool, Arsenal, Luton, Cardiff, Bolton Wanderers, East Fife and Partick Thistle during the war years. Highlights of Shankly's wartime football career were the 1941 War Cup final against Arsenal at Wembley, which Preston won after a replay, and captaining Scotland in a wartime international.

After playing in nearly every game for Arsenal during one of the wartime cup competitions, Shankly was rather aggrieved to be dropped for the final against Charlton Athletic at Wembley. Arsenal had most of their players available for the game and Shankly was not selected for the final, their own registered players taking precedence. Shankly regarded this as an injustice and, despite Arsenal's attempts to placate him with a cash and ticket payment, the dejected Scot trooped out of Highbury handing back the 'sweetener' on his way out. Shankly made a mental note that if he were ever in a position to select a team, it would be solely on ability, with sentiment never allowed into the equation. Joe Mercer remembered the incident when interviewed in the 1970s. He recalls: *'He would get terribly upset over injustices and matters of principle. I remember one day he was terribly worked up. He played for Arsenal during the war and I met him outside Wembley when they played Charlton in the wartime cup final. Bill had played right through the competition but George Male had arrived home and they picked him instead of Bill. He was most indignant and his language was dreadful.'*

Shankly, in fact, decided to stand on the terraces to watch the game, which Arsenal won 7-1.

Shankly's posting to Glasgow was to prove a happy and eventful period in his life. It was while stationed there that he met his future wife, Nessie, who was in the WRAF at the same camp. Nessie first spotted Bill jogging around the camp and, knowing nothing about football, made enquiries about the strange man who appeared to be permanently training. The information that he was Bill Shankly, a famous international footballer, meant little to her but within a short period of time they got to know each other and, in 1944, they married in Nessie's home town of Glasgow. In his autobiography, Shankly revealed that he would often woo Nessie with toasted cheese that he took over from his section to hers. In later years, when Bill moved to football management, the Shankly family had to undergo a considerable amount of upheaval moving from one area of the country to another as Shankly changed jobs in the management merry-go-round before settling on Merseyside. Whatever career move Bill made, it was with the full support of Nessie, who always provided a strong and stable family environment while allowing her husband to devote an enormous amount of his time and energy to building and developing whatever football club was receiving his service at the time.

While stationed in Glasgow, Shankly signed to play for Partick Thistle and apart from providing him with a good standard of football, he was eternally grateful to them for paying all expenses when he had an operation on his knee. It was an injury that Shankly had been carrying for some time but to him injuries did not exist and he had chosen to ignore it. The medical attention he finally succumbed to revealed that he had been playing for a long period of time with badly displaced cartilage. In his later years as a manager, he demanded this same level of courage and toughness from his players and, as Gerry Byrne's incredible FA Cup final display against Leeds in 1965 showed, he usually got it. After regaining his fitness, Shankly continued to play for Partick Thistle until he was demobbed in January 1946.

Shankly's first game on his return to Preston was an FA Cup tie against Everton that was to be played over two legs. Shankly won the game for Preston with an extra-time penalty kick at Goodison Park. Although finishing the season without honours, the North End faithful were richly entertained by a player Shankly regarded as a football genius, Tom Finney. Nicknamed the 'Preston Plumber', Finney's game did not have a weakness. He was skilful with both feet, strong in a tackle and a brilliant header of the ball. Finney is regarded by many soccer pundits as the only genuine challenger to George Best as the greatest all-round soccer talent of the post-war years in Britain. Later, Shankly would never tire of telling his players at Liverpool about the great Tom Finney: *He was so good that the opposition would have a man marking him in the pre-match warm up!* And if any of his Liverpool players got a little bit too big for their boots, Shankly would soon bring them down a notch with a curt *'Tom Finney could play better than you with his overcoat on!'*

If Finney made an immediate impression on Shankly, the feeling was mutual, with the young Preston player being particularly struck by Shankly's incredible enthusiasm and will to win. During Finney's home debut for Preston, he remembers being constantly urged by Shankly to 'keep on trying, we can still win'. The fact that Preston were four down with just a few minutes to play meant nothing to the indomitable Scot. Within a short period, Finney's talent made him a marked man, with opposing defenders trying every trick in the book, including threats of physical violence. On one occasion, Shankly overheard a seasoned professional threatening Finney with a broken leg. Shankly sidled up to the player in question and in no uncertain terms told him that if he broke Finney's leg, then Shankly would break his. With Shankly's ultimatum in mind, the player had second thoughts and did not bother Finney again for the rest of the game.

The late 1940s saw Shankly playing his final couple of seasons for Preston, who were still regarded as one of the most entertaining teams in the country. After a defeat at Highbury, which saw league leaders Arsenal increase their lead over third-placed Preston in

February 1948, Preston chairman James Taylor, a man Shankly greatly admired, commented *'I don't mind if we lose so long as the team serves up first-class football!'*

Shankly's incredible fitness impressed Edgar Turner of the *Sporting Chronicle* who, after witnessing the Preston captain, now well into his thirties, clinch a victory over Chelsea at Deepdale, commented: *'It was human dynamo Bill Shankly who scored Preston's second from the penalty spot. How Shankly keeps it up game after game, year after year, I don't know. He's been with Preston fifteen seasons now and is playing as well as ever.'* Speaking to the *Sporting Chronicle* in 1948, after playing his 290th league game for Preston, Shankly rejected rumours that he was about to retire when he told John Graydon: *'I'd be grateful, John, if you would deny a report that I'm thinking of retiring. Some people seem to think I'm a veteran because I have been playing for many seasons. I'm only thirty-four, and you don't call that old, do you? I intend to go on playing as long as possible and my great ambition is to captain Preston at Wembley.'* Graydon backed up Shankly's statement that he was far from finished by citing a recent game against Arsenal, after which Graydon wrote: *'On his form against Arsenal, Bill Shankly, with Archie MacCauley and Arsenal's Joe Mercer, again showed how to play artistic football without wasting energy, and many of Shankly's along-the-carpet passes might have brought goals had Preston had a more forceful centre forward.'*

Shankly's wish to captain Preston at Wembley looked like it would be fulfilled in 1948 when a McIntosh goal against Manchester City at Maine Road gave them a quarter-final game, again at Maine Road, against Manchester United. Preston, under the guidance of Shankly and Bobbie Beattie, their two most experienced campaigners, were confident that this was their year for the FA Cup. However, Manchester United, under the inspired captaincy of Johnny Carey, knocked Preston out and went on to win the cup that year.

The following season, 1948/49, was to be Shankly's last at the Lancashire club. No longer able to command a regular first-team place, Shankly was on the lookout for a new opportunity in football

Shankly duels with Lishman of Arsenal, Highbury, 1949.

and, despite his previous claims that he was not thinking of retiring from the playing side, it had always been obvious, particularly to his peers, that Shankly was prime managerial material. With Preston struggling to avoid relegation, Shankly was brought back into the team during the early months of 1949. With star player Finney suffering a series of injuries that kept him out of the team that season, Preston were fighting a losing battle to retain their First Division status.

3

INTO MANAGEMENT

Word that Shankly was looking for a new opportunity reached Third Division Carlisle United, who were keen to fill the managerial vacancy at the club with a young 'tracksuit' manager. After meeting the Carlisle board, the Cumbrian club offered their ex-player his first managerial position. They also offered wages that were the equivalent of what he was receiving at Preston and, coupled with the fact that Carlisle was only a few hours from Glasgow, which would allow Nessie to see her family in Scotland more often, the offer to take over at Carlisle held considerable appeal to Shankly.

When he informed Preston of his decision, they did not react favourably. Although he was no longer a first-team regular, they were obviously keen to hang on to all of their experienced players in their fight against relegation. A benefit game was offered as an incentive to stay but Shankly, after giving the club sixteen years of loyal service, was under the impression that a benefit match would be awarded to him regardless of whether he stayed with the club or not. The dilemma for Shankly was that if he did not accept the managerial opportunity that had presented itself, another might not emerge for a long time. He decided to stand by his decision to leave Preston but was embittered by the fact that a benefit match was no longer on offer. Up to this point, Shankly had regarded joining

Preston in 1933 as the greatest football decision of his life and could not have been happier. Although his departure from Preston had not been as amicable as he had hoped, it was not a rift that lasted for any great length of time (as Shankly's dealings in the transfer market with the Deepdale club in the 1960s would bear out). Just as Shankly's name as a manager would always be synonymous with Liverpool FC, Shankly's playing career will always be intrinsically linked to Preston North End. Just three matches short of his 300th league game for Preston, Shankly played his final game for them on 19 March 1949 against Sunderland at Deepdale. A notable record that Shankly created at Preston was 43 successive FA Cup ties for one club.

Although Shankly accepted the Carlisle post on 22 March, contractual difficulties with Preston still had to be sorted out and his first game in charge at Carlisle was not until 4 April, which was the Cumberland Cup final against Workington, with Carlisle winning 2-1. His first league game as Carlisle manager was on 9 April, at home to Tranmere, the game resulting in a 2-2 draw. Right from the outset, he immersed himself totally in all aspects of running the club. He was to claim in later years that he had been preparing himself throughout his playing career for the day when he would move into football management. Now he had the opportunity to put everything he had learnt into practice.

One of the first things Shankly set about achieving at Carlisle was to create an atmosphere of pride in the club. He ordered new kit for his players, helped to tidy up the rapidly deteriorating terracing and stand and he even mucked in with the junior players, helping them to brush out the dressing rooms and polish the first team's boots. If a job needed doing, Shankly did it with them. With a new air of optimism about the club, results and attendances began to improve.

One of Shankly's first signings at Carlisle was his former teammate at Preston, Paddy Waters. The Dublin born wing half had been struggling to regain his first-team place at Preston after injury and Shankly offered him a new start at Carlisle. Initially Waters was not keen to sign as he revealed in *The Carlisle United Story*: 'I took *one look at Brunton Park and had one thing on my mind... what time is the first train back to Lancashire? It was just like a big, wooden, rabbit hutch. The facilities were shocking, especially for someone like me who'd been used to Preston's ground.'* With Shankly's formidable powers of persuasion to the fore, however, Waters decided to sign and he went on to serve Carlisle with distinction for the next eight years. One of Waters' strongest memories of Shankly at Carlisle was the marvellous atmosphere that he seemed to generate: *'There was always a great team spirit at Carlisle and always a competition to keep your place. Shankly always had a strong reserve team wherever he's been and it makes for a very determined side. It was just the same at Carlisle in the early 1950s. The place was really buzzing while Shanks was in charge. He lived for football – football mad.'*

It is interesting to note that Shankly's tactic of rubbishing the opposition, which was used to such good effect during his pre-match pep talks at Liverpool, was employed by him right from the start of his managerial career at Carlisle. Paddy Waters recalled the air of excitement around Brunton Park when the players heard that they had been drawn to play cup-holders Arsenal in the FA Cup during the 1950/51 season. Shankly, however, soon put a stop to the euphoria when he summoned his players together before the following day's training: *'Arsenal, who the hell are they? I've never heard of them'* he quipped before putting his players through their morning session.

On the day of the match, Shankly sent out his team to play their illustrious opponents at Highbury, determined not to be overawed by either the opposition or the occasion. The ploy worked and Carlisle brought off the shock of the day, holding Arsenal to a 0-0 draw. Hopes were high that Carlisle could finish off the job in the replay and the team's confidence was further boosted when Shankly rushed into the dressing room, shut the door and excitedly told them: *'Boys, I've just seen them getting out of their coach. They should be in hospital. They're in a right state. The centre forward can hardly walk.'* Like many a Liverpool team a decade later, the Carlisle players ran out onto the pitch thinking they were about to take on a bunch of half-fit has-beens. In the early part of the game, the Shankly tactic worked with Carlisle more than holding their own. The turning point of the game, however, was when a strong challenge from one of the tough-tackling Arsenal defenders effectively put Carlisle's danger man, winger Billy Hogan, out of the match. After this incident, Arsenal's class began to tell and, in the end, they ran out comfortable 4-1 winners.

It was at Carlisle that he first began to harness the Shankly master plan of the fans and the club being one. When an opposition eleven stepped out to play a Shankly team, they weren't taking on eleven players but the club as a whole. Within a short space of time, Shankly became a firm favourite with the Carlisle supporters. Before every home game, he would speak to them over the tannoy, explaining the reasons behind any team changes and giving summaries of how the club had been playing in away matches. As was the case with practically every player who was fortunate to have him as a manager, the Carlisle players, particularly the younger ones, were totally bowled over by the infectious enthusiasm of their new manager. Average players were made to feel like internationals; to the young players he was something of a father figure.

In his autobiography, Shankly spoke of the style of management he set out to achieve and described how he hoped to treat his players: *'I was determined to be fair with them, instead of victimising them, punishing them, fining them, castigating them or humiliating them at the wrong time or in front of the wrong people. I would not have favourites. A player could be my biggest enemy but if he could play I would say he was great. If he didn't like me, it didn't make any difference to my judgement. Throughout my time at Preston I saw favouritism. "Jimmy is a nice little chap" they said, so Jimmy would play even though he wasn't as good a player as Peter. I saw that happening and I saw it was wrong.'* Throughout his managerial career, Shankly stuck to the man-management blueprint that he devised at Carlisle and it was a plan that would be a crucial element in the creation of his great Liverpool teams.

After two happy seasons at Brunton Park, during which he took them to the brink of promotion to the Second Division, Shankly applied for the vacant manager's job at Grimsby Town. Lack of finance to back the ambitious Shankly was always going to be a problem at Carlisle but Grimsby, who had recently been relegated to the Third Division, impressed Shankly as a club with First Division potential. Shankly had, in fact, first been approached by Grimsby in the spring of 1951, when he was offered the coach's position at Blundell Park. Carlisle, keen to hold on to the man who was breathing new life into the club, increased his salary to ward off the Grimsby advances. When Charles Spencer resigned as the Grimsby manager at the end of the 1950/51 season, however, the Grimsby board knew the man they wanted and were delighted when Shankly accepted their offer.

Although both the club and its supporters, many of whom remembered losing Shankly as a player to Preston in 1933, were deeply unhappy at his decision to leave Carlisle, it was with their good wishes that he left Brunton Park and the club that launched him into professional football as both a player and a manager. The vacant manager's post at Carlisle was taken by Fred Emery, but Shankly was obviously a hard act to follow, as former international footballer and later renowned sports journalist Ivor Broadis once remarked: *'Following Bill Shankly at Carlisle with his match-day talk to the fans over the loud speaker system must have been like following Sammy Davis at the London Palladium.'*

When Shankly arrived at Grimsby, the squad of players he had to work with was somewhat depleted after the sale of some of the club's better players. After making some astute moves into the transfer market, Shankly quickly built a talented team of players who had proven league experience. He quickly had them playing as a unit and the team narrowly missed out on promotion to the Second Division in his first season at the club. Employing the same type of training methods that he had begun at Carlisle, with the emphasis on ball work, teamwork, and set-piece plays, the Grimsby team once again pushed hard for promotion during the 1952/53 season but fell away towards the end of the campaign, finishing fifth in the league.

With the Grimsby team in need of an injection of new players and not a great deal of money available to bring them to Blundell Park, Shankly felt he was not in a position to improve the Humberside club's prospects and took up an offer from Workington to help them avoid losing their Football League status. After guiding Grimsby to victory over Tranmere Rovers during the 1953 Christmas and Boxing Day games, Shankly resigned as Grimsby manager and took over at Workington on 6 January 1954. An added incentive to Shankly was the promise of a bonus payment if he saved the club from going out of the League. When Shankly arrived at the Third Division (North) club, they were in a desperate position. Their previous manager, Ted Smith, had left football to take up the offer of employment in the prison service and the managerless team were lying at the bottom of the division. Tommy Jones, who was club coach at Workington, was doing his best to get the club away from the foot of the table but it was clear that strong managerial direction was needed to help stem the tide of poor results. With the arrival of Shankly and the boost of new players at the club, most of whom were signed by the Workington board before Shankly's arrival, the team began to show an improvement in form and finished the season a couple of places clear of the dreaded re-election zone.

A couple of items of information about Workington that Shankly had not been informed of at his interview for the job were that the club still had gas lighting and Workington Rugby League team also trained and played their home games on the same Borough Park pitch that the football team played on. The churning-up of the pitch by the rugby team did not go down at all well with Shankly!

As was the case with every club he was involved with, Shankly became involved with all aspects of running the club at Workington. A great deal of his free time was spent fund-raising or organising Sunday morning training sessions for the youth team. What Shankly had not yet developed was his rapport with the press and media that was so marked during the Liverpool years. When members of the local press arrived at the ground to try to get an interview with the Workington boss, they would be sent away empty handed after being informed that he was involved in a tactical talk with the team, or he was out on his daily jog. Likewise, if they called at his house, he would either be in the bath or out training.

Shankly spent the summer months at Workington restructuring his playing staff and set out to build a team who would be capable of putting in a challenge for promotion to the Second Division. Just as he had at his two previous clubs, Shankly introduced new training methods which were designed not only to get the players super-fit but also to build up team spirit. Players who played under Shankly at Workington were amazed at how quickly Shankly was able to get them to regard training as an enjoyable experience rather than a chore. He even introduced an end of training five-a-side, which was always the married men against the bachelors, with Shankly captain of the married men. From all accounts the ribbing between the teams helped to create a bond of comradeship that pulled the players together. Inspired by the Shankly magic, Workington began the 1954/55 season with a flourish and at the beginning of December were just 4 points off the top spot in the League. The team was playing good, entertaining football and the general atmosphere at Borough Park was one of optimism. The second round of the FA Cup also brought a result and a chance meeting that delighted and inspired Shankly and his Workington players.

Workington were drawn away to Leyton Orient, who were doing well near the top of Division Three (South). Shankly and his team set off the evening before the match to catch the midday Flying Scotsman to London. Once settled on the train Shankly got word that the legendary Hungarian team of Puskas, Kocsis and company were also on the train, travelling back to London after defeating Shankly's beloved Scotland 4-2 at Hampden Park. Shankly lost no time in telling his players to follow him and to make the acquaintance of a team that were widely regarded as the greatest team in the world. The Hungarians were only too happy to exchange pleasantries with the Workington team and both sets of players conversed, as best they could, for the remainder of the journey. Shankly, in fact, obtained the signatures of the Hungarian team on a postcard and it was a memento of the occasion that he would always treasure. On reaching London, the two teams said their goodbyes and Workington set off to take on Leyton Orient.

Workington, obviously drawing inspiration from their chance meeting with the Hungarian legends, won with a goal from Bertolini. The celebrations at Borough Park were complete when a postcard arrived from the Hungarian FA congratulating Workington on their *'historic win over Leyton Orient.'*

Workington's cup run came to an end in the next round when Luton overwhelmed them 5-0. Their league form also became inconsistent but they still managed to finish a creditable eighth. Before the season was over, Shankly began to prepare for the following season's campaign. Always on the lookout for young talent, he placed an advert in the local press advising all young foot-ballers in the county to write to him and he would fix them up with a trial. In fact, his youth policy blossomed to such an extent that the reserve team were now known as the 'Shankly Babes' and were drawing crowds of 2,000-plus at home games.

The start of the 1955/56 season saw Workington once again riding high near the top of the league and expectations were high that the team would be able to sustain their promotion challenge during this campaign. The beginning of November saw them defeating Barrow 6-1 but, a week later, the club was brought down to earth with a 5-1 defeat at Accrington Stanley, followed a few days later by the body blow of Shankly deciding to take up the offer of the assistant manager's post at Huddersfield Town. The offer had been put to Shankly by his former Preston teammate Andy Beattie, who was manager at Huddersfield. Shankly, who had no contract at Workington, had found managing the West Cumberland team a hard but enjoyable experience. The club was being run on a shoe-string and had to depend on donations from its Auxiliary Association Supporters Club and other fund-raising activities for its survival. The boardroom wrangling at Workington was always a source of amusement to Shankly and he once commented that to witness the arguments and resignations that seemed to take place every week was *'better than going to the pictures'*. Even after his departure from Borough Park, Shankly kept in touch with goings-on at the club through correspondence with club groundsman, Billy

Watson. Shankly would often enquire after the board members and would give them nicknames similar to the names of American gangsters from the prohibition era. One board member, Jack Wannop, was always referred to as Johnny Bunny, one of Al Capone's notorious henchmen.

The impact that Shankly had on Workington and the players who were members of Shankly's team at Borough Park can be gauged from a series of interviews with former Workington players who played under him, conducted by Martin Wingfield for his book *So Sad, So Very Sad…The League History of Workington AFC* (1992). Ted Cushin recalled: *'He had the ability to make his players feel ten feet tall. He never shouted at a player, indeed rarely raised his voice at all - except to blame the referee!'* Rex Dunlop is another former Workington player on whom Shankly made a deep impression: *'He was a tremendous motivator and had a great sense of humour. On one occasion after beating high-flying Barnsley 2-0 at Borough Park he turned and said 'I wish to hell we would play like them!'* Jack Vitty, who was appointed team captain by Shankly recalled: *'A local firm, the Tognarelli family, who specialised in ice-cream production, gave an 'Ice-cream Ball' for the Workington players and wives at the Central Hotel, where Shankly was staying having just taken up the post of Workington manager. Shanks displayed his well-known aversion to anything not connected to football by keeping guard in the hotel foyer until the end of the function, instead of retiring to bed at 10.30 as usual. The players all felt that 'Big Brother' was watching them - but he failed to detect the odd drink hidden behind potted palms!'*

One Workington player who did fall foul of Shankly's no-alcohol policy, however, was Ernie Whittle. Whittle, a player whose skill and goalscoring ability were regarded by Shankly as one of the main reasons for Workington avoiding the drop out of the Football League, had a few too many after one game and news of Ernie's breaching the Shankly code of conduct reached his teetotal boss. Whittle was summoned into Shankly's office and was fined a week's wages. Later in the day, however, Shankly discovered that Whittle, who was one of only a small number of English players with the Cumbrian club, had recently been on the receiving end of what was intended as good-natured ribbing from the Scottish contingent at the club. To Ernie it was all getting rather tiresome and he had decided to drown his sorrows with a few pints. With this in mind, Shankly decided to pay Whittle a visit. He then told a bewildered Whittle to get into the car with him and proceeded to drive the player to the nearest shopping centre. Still not knowing the purpose of his unexpected visit to town, Whittle was taken by Shankly to a local tailors shop, where a new suit was purchased for him by his idiosyncratic manager. It is highly likely that the cost of the new suit was probably greater than the week's wages that Shankly had fined the player but to Shankly it was probably his way of showing a player he held in high regard that he knew what he was going through and that he was not on his own. To this day it is a gesture that Whittle has not forgotten.

Billy Watson, the Workington groundsman, with whom Shankly struck up an immediate friendship, recalled the afternoon tea breaks in the boiler room with Shankly: *'I can still hear his steel-tipped heels as he walked down the tunnel. He would pull up a lemonade crate to sit on and I would say to myself in anticipation, 'What will he reminisce about today?' Would it be his own Tom Finney, or maybe West Brom's Ronnie Starling with his emerald green overcoat. Maybe it would be that auto-graphed postcard from the world-beating Hungarian team he met on the train when the Reds went to Leyton Orient and defeated them in the FA Cup. He treasured that. His marvellous laugh as he tells me yet again about the old lady in Cleaton Moor trying to hit him with her walking stick and shouting 'Get back to Workington!' because his 'A' team had just beaten her beloved Cleaton Moor Celtic. You can't buy memories like that.'*

Although unhappy to see him leave, the Workington board wished Shankly well and, according to all accounts, it was an amicable parting; a fact borne out twenty-five years later when he returned to Borough Park in August 1980 to open the 'Shankly Lounge'.

Shankly's task at Huddersfield was to help Andy Beattie pull the club away from the foot of the First Division. He was also given the task of developing the club's youth policy. Despite the presence of

Shankly, Huddersfield failed to avoid relegation to the Second Division at the end of the 1955/56 season.

The start of the new season saw Shankly still in charge of the reserve team and among the fine crop of youngsters that were being groomed by Shankly for the first team were future England internationals Ray Wilson and Mike O'Grady, plus a fifteen-year-old Scot who, with Wilson, would develop into one of the game's greats: Denis Law. Law was already on Huddersfield's books when Shankly arrived at the club but had yet to sign professional terms. It was obvious to Shankly from his first look at Law in action that the club had an incredible player on their hands but the Scottish youth was so frail – weighing less than seven stone – that Shankly put him on a steak and milk diet in an attempt to build him up. Recalling his first sight of Denis Law, Shankly later wrote in his autobiography: *'Right from the start Dennis stood out with his enthusiasm and will to win - nastiness, if you like. He would have died to have won. He had a temper and was a terror – a bloody terror, with ability.'* Shankly was also grooming future England international Ray Wilson during this period and was responsible for Wilson's conversion from a wing half into a full-back. Interviewed by Ken Rogers for his book *Everton Greats* (1989), Wilson recalled his former manager at Huddersfield: *'I remember Bill Shankly's five-a-side games at Huddersfield. He would keep four Scots to make up his side against five Englishmen. It was England v. Scotland on the asphalt car park at Leeds Road under the mill and the gasometer. We would keep playing until Scotland got in front and that was that!'* Despite the image that Shankly would often project as the tough Scot who stood no nonsense, Wilson remembers Shankly differently: *'People talk about Shankly being a hard man. In my experience he found it difficult to come down on people. He played the role of his favourite film star, James Cagney. The little tough guy. Deep down he was not a tough individual himself. It was just enthusiasm with Bill, almost a boyish approach to the game he loved.'* Denis Law, remembering Shankly from this period, recalled that Shankly would always fill him with confidence and make him feel cocky. *'Forget your strengths, work on your weaknesses'* he would constantly tell him.

During the early part of the 1956/57 season, Shankly's reserve team were going well and some of the Shankly youngsters were pushing for first-team places. In contrast, the Huddersfield first team had made an unconvincing start to the campaign and, after three successive defeats, Andy Beattie resigned the manager's position and Shankly took over on 5 November 1956. Although Shankly was happy now to be in charge of a club of Huddersfield Town's calibre, taking over from his friend Andy Beattie was always a source of embarrassment to him. The ideal situation to him would have been a partnership but it was not to be and, although uneasy about taking the place of his great pal at the helm of Huddersfield, it did not hinder their friendship, which lasted throughout Shankly's Liverpool years.

With Shankly now in charge, initial results were promising but a four-match losing run leading up to the Christmas fixtures revealed to Shankly that regaining their First Division status was not going to be easy. Shankly had by now introduced several of his teenage prodigies into the first team and was delighted to see Denis Law score his first league goal for the club against Notts County on Boxing Day, 1956. Shankly was also pleased to see a man who will always be a folk hero on Merseyside, Dave Hickson, hitting the net regularly for Town. However, the season ended in disappointment for Huddersfield, who could only finish in mid-table.

Ray Wilson remembers a game during his time playing for Huddersfield when Charlton were leading 4-0 at half-time, with Huddersfield pinned in their penalty area for most of the first forty-five minutes. As the despondent team sat in the dressing room, Shankly applied his famous psychology: *'Four breakaways, that's all they've had. Now in the second half you'll murder them!'*

The following season saw Shankly and Huddersfield involved in two major fights: one to gain promotion, the other to hang on to Denis Law. Law was by now seventeen and had yet to sign as a professional with the club. Most of the top clubs in Britain were now on the trail of the teenage sensation and it looked likely that Huddersfield would lose him. It was only after much persuasion by

Shankly that  Denis Law finally decided to sign himself to Huddersfield Town. As players who joined Liverpool in later years would confirm, when Shankly was in full flow, he was an expert at coaxing players to sign on the dotted line.

Even with Law in the team, Huddersfield failed to maintain a promotion push and finished a disappointing ninth in the League. It was obvious that, despite the fact that Huddersfield was a team sprinkled with fine young players, money was needed to buy that extra class to turn them into a promotion-winning team. All through his managerial career, Shankly knew it was not good enough having ambition without ammunition. He had enormous self belief that he would eventually produce a trophy-winning team but he needed a board with the will and the finances to back him. The club that would do just that, Liverpool, were about to give him the call. The beginning of the 1959/60 season saw Huddersfield make a bright start with five wins out of their first seven games. They then went through an inconsistent spell and it was obvious to Shankly that, unless the club allowed him to strengthen the team, promotion would not be forthcoming.

After a poor home performance against Cardiff City, which saw them lose 1-0, he was approached by Liverpool chairman Tom Williams and director Harry Latham. After exchanging pleasantries they asked Shankly if he would be interested in taking over the best team in the country. Shankly replied *'I didn't know Matt Busby had retired from Manchester United!'* Nevertheless, Shankly was interested,

Bill Shankly plays Sunday afternoon football with the kids and dads at Huddersfield. Shankly carried on this tradition with the children and parents who lived near his Liverpool home until his death in 1981.

for he knew of the untapped potential that existed at Anfield. Liverpool was a big city club just waiting for a messiah to transform it from a slumbering giant into a football institution. Shankly was later to claim that it was his destiny to go to Liverpool.

Although Shankly did not relish the thought of having to leave behind the youngsters he had been grooming for stardom, such as Law and Wilson, the temptation to join Liverpool was too strong and after his last game in charge of Huddersfield, ironically against Liverpool on 28 November 1959, Shankly decided to accept Liverpool's offer.

If Shankly's decision was probably the most significant in the history of Liverpool Football Club, it tuned out to be a catastrophic one for Huddersfield Town. It may be conjecture but it seems highly likely that if finance had been made available to Shankly, and taking into consideration the talented youngsters that Huddersfield had at their disposal, the incredible success that Liverpool were to achieve under Shankly could surely have been, at the very least, partly emulated by the Yorkshire club. Perhaps Huddersfield Town supporters did not have the potential to be moulded into anything like the 'Red Army' at Anfield that was so crucial to Liverpool's success, but it is possible that Town, with Shankly at the helm, could have at least enjoyed the same level of success that their Yorkshire rivals, Leeds United, achieved in the 1960s and '70s. On leaving Huddersfield to become Liverpool's manager, he told his players: *'I'm going to a place where they live, eat, sleep and drink football. And that's my place.'*

4

THE PLACE WHERE THEY LIVE, EAT, SLEEP AND DRINK FOOTBALL

Bill Shankly was once asked to describe what he found at Liverpool when he arrived in December 1959. His reply was, as ever, blunt and honest: *'Quite candidly, it was a shambles of a place. The team wasn't very good; the ground was run down and wasn't good enough for the team and the supporters.'*

But he had played at Anfield many times while a player at Preston and sensed that Liverpool had the capability to be a footballing force: *'I could sense the potential among the crowd. I'd played here and the people were fantastic. They wanted to see their team back in the First Division; they were desperate for success. It was all there waiting to be directed. Liverpool was a city of a million people with a deep love of football. The potential was tremendous and that is why I came to Anfield. I was only interested in one thing, success for the club; which meant success for the people. I wanted to make the people happy.'*

As the years unfolded, Shankly did indeed make the people happy. No manager of a football club had ever had before, or probably ever will have again, a closer relationship with his club's supporters. It was once quite aptly described as a 'marriage made in heaven'. *'I'd been at Celtic-Rangers games and seen the fans kissing the team bus. The people are the same kind of people as me. They are passionate about football'* he said.

That Bill Shankly came to Liverpool in the first place was due largely to club chairman T.V. Williams. Williams, like Shankly, was

The new Liverpool manager attends a function with Anfield legend Billy Liddell, Liverpool chairman T.V. Williams and the Lord Mayor of Liverpool, 1961.

known as a man of integrity, with much warmth and dignity, and like the tough Scot, he could be short-tempered as well. Williams had spotted something in Shankly when he encountered him over the years. Shankly had actually first applied for the manager's job at Liverpool in the early 1950s but had failed to get the appointment. Years later Williams persuaded the rest of the Liverpool board that Shankly had the potential to take the club back into the First Division, and after getting assurance from Williams that he would have sole control over team selection, Shankly agreed to take the job.

Prior to Shankly's arrival at the club, successive managers had to have their team selection checked by the boardroom for approval, a situation he couldn't tolerate. He was happy though with the backroom staff already in place at the club, demanding loyalty from them which they eagerly gave, and he returned to them the same loyalty and respect. Joe Fagan was at the club about a year before the human tornado, Shankly, swept in. He recalls: *'We were going nowhere, but the whole club changed when Bill arrived. It started to vibrate. Everything started to move forward for Liverpool. It was his great personality. A beam shone out of him. The other thing about him was that he was a simple man. There was nothing pretentious about him. Bill Shankly was undoubtedly Liverpool's greatest ever signing.'*

As Joe Fagan says, Shankly did have an incredible ability to appear both magical and ordinary at the same time. Bob Paisley (who during the Shankly years at Anfield held the positions of reserve-team trainer, physiotherapist, coach and assistant manager, before taking over from Shankly and becoming the most successful manager in British football history) also remembered Shankly's arrival at Anfield: *'When Bill came to Liverpool, a friend at Huddersfield told me I'd never be able to work with Bill for more than two years. I wouldn't be able to stand the strain, he said. But from the moment he arrived, we got on like a house on fire. Bill was happy with us and we were certainly happy with him. He carried us along through the sheer force of his personality.'*

Shankly's managerial route to Liverpool had been auspicious, and he had certainly had to learn the hard way about what a demanding job running a club on a shoestring budget can be. After periods at Carlisle, Grimsby and Workington, he finally moved up the football ladder as assistant to first-team boss Andy Beattie at Huddersfield, a club with a great history but who were struggling, unsuccessfully as it turned out, to avoid relegation to the Second Division. Eventually, Shankly took over from Beattie as first-team manager, but was unsuccessful in his attempt to get Huddersfield back into the top flight.

After taking over at Liverpool, Shankly faced initially the same major dilemma as he had done at Huddersfield: it was no good having ambition without ammunition, and he needed money to buy players. It was as simple as that, and unsuccessful bids were made to bring Jack Charlton and Scottish midfield dynamo Dave Mackay to the club. Shankly had been told by the Liverpool board when he had taken the manager's job that they were as ambitious for success as he was, but during his early period at the club, he began to doubt this. The question started to play on Shankly's mind: should he have stayed at Huddersfield Town?

Anfield and the club's training ground at Melwood were also of a very poor standard for a club that was supposedly ambitious. Bill's wife, Nessie, was happy at Huddersfield and admits that during their early days on Merseyside there was much soul-searching being done by her husband. *'The Liverpool people couldn't have been warmer or more welcoming'*, she said. *'The club, however, was a big disappointment to Bill. The biggest shock of all to him was the training ground at Melwood. I remember we were standing in the middle of the pitch at Melwood and Bill said to me, "Oh Ness, have I made a terrible mistake leaving Huddersfield?" He thought at that moment that coming to Liverpool was a big mistake because the conditions at the training ground were so appalling. Nobody would believe it. Bill had a battle on his hands. He would go there every day with Bob Paisley, Reuben Bennett, Joe Fagan and the groundsman at Melwood, Eli Wass, and they were digging up the place with their bare hands. There were bricks and stones everywhere. All there was was a dirty little hut where the players changed. There was no running water. Anfield wasn't much better. It was a nice ground, but rather dilapidated at that time. There was no water supply for the pitch, so they had to get cracking on that, get in touch with the council and get a water supply into the ground. It all took a long time.'*

On the playing side, the arrival of Shankly at Liverpool resulted in them putting in a spirited effort to catch the clubs chasing a promotion spot, although they could only finish in third place. There was now, however, a buzz about the club, and Liverpool's captain at the time, Ronnie Moran, who has served the club with distinction and loyalty as both a player and member of the backroom staff since the beginning of the Shankly years, once explained: *'I learned more in the first three months than I'd done in the seven years that I'd been a pro. I wish I'd been five years younger.'* Shankly used that first season at the club to assess the players he had at his disposal. *'After a couple of months, I knew who I thought could play and who couldn't. That was my first priority at Anfield, to get to know the people I was working*

Shankly prepares to put his team through their paces at Liverpool's Melwood training ground.

with. I had to assess the whole place, the directors as well', he said. His assessment of the club's directors left him with the uncomfortable feeling that obtaining financial backing to bring in new blood was going to be a struggle. He once declared: *'At a football club, there's a holy trinity; the players, the manager and the supporters. Directors don't come into it. They are only there to sign the cheques; not to make them out. We'll do that – they just sign them.'*

41

An early shot of Roger Hunt at Melwood. Hunt became an Anfield legend during the Shankly years, with the Kop dubbing him 'Sir Roger'. Hunt scored 285 goals for Liverpool and was a member of England's victorious World Cup team in 1966.

Shankly's first full season at the club, 1960/61, saw them once again finish in third spot. He was now desperate for someone in a position of authority at the club to 'sign the cheques'. Fortunately for Shankly, that man had now arrived. *'Eric Sawyer was the beginning of Liverpool'*, Shankly claimed. *'He was willing to spend money. He said to me, "If you can get the players, I'll get you the money."'*

Sawyer, an accountant and key figure in charge of finance at the Littlewoods Pools organisation, was placed on the board at Liverpool at the behest of Littlewoods' founding figure, John Moores. Moores was now chairman at Everton and, after pumping substantial amounts of money into the club, was about to preside over the re-emergence of Everton as a force in British football. Moores also had substantial shares in Liverpool Football Club and

The great Billy Liddell. His Liverpool career was near its end when Shankly became manager in 1959.

this entitled him to place a nominee on the board at Anfield – that man was Eric Sawyer. Sawyer, unlike the majority of directors that Shankly had had to deal with in his football career, wasn't interested in telling him who should or shouldn't be in the team. The Liverpool boss could now spend the summer months of 1961 plotting Liverpool's all-out push for promotion in a more optimistic frame of mind. But he still had to face the wrath of the shareholders before the new season began.

5

PROMOTION OR BUST

To accuse Bill Shankly of instructing his players not to try during a game of football is akin to suggesting that George Best has been celibate for the past thirty years. But incredibly, this accusation was put to the Liverpool manager during a heated post-mortem after another disappointing season at Anfield. Liverpool's failure to gain promotion in 1961 led to ructions at the club's annual meeting of shareholders. Both the chairman, T.V. Williams, and Shankly came under heavy criticism from an irate group of shareholders, who demanded to know why the team had finished as Second Division also-rans yet again.

'*Tell me, Mr Shankly*', enquired Solly Isenwater, who was chairman of the Shareholders Association, '*is it true that you have ever said that when the team were leading by one or two clear goals, they could take it easy, and not get injured?*' A seething Shankly got to his feet and replied: '*That's rubbish. I have never heard anything so silly.*' Fighting hard to keep his anger under control, he went on. '*I think the tension on players is too much for them to carry. It's not created by one or two failures to gain promotion, but by the past seven seasons.*'

Not satisfied by his reply, one of the shareholders expressed the view that some of the players were just not good enough and that money must be spent to bring in new talent. T.V. Williams told the meeting that the directors were making continuous efforts to obtain players and could have spent millions if Liverpool's bids had been accepted. *'Players are refusing to come to Liverpool. We've been up and down the country, day and night, looking for players, but they preferred London where they still thought the streets were paved with gold'*, he said. *'Is Goodison Park in London, because they seem to get the players all right'*, another unhappy shareholder sarcastically responded. Returning to the point made earlier in the meeting about Liverpool players' lack of effort, Solly Isenwater remarked: *'The board should have taken action to show supporters that no Liverpool player could just stop playing in the middle of a game. Certainly no member of the board, or any businessman, would allow an employee to stop work as and when he pleased.'* Williams reiterated Shankly's reply to this question and informed Isenwater that he was *'talking a lot of nonsense'*. *'And in any case, why should you know?'* the short-tempered chairman responded. This brought an angry response from many of the shareholders and a proposed vote of no confidence in the chair was averted only after a period of cooling down.

One thing was made patently obvious to Shankly, who must have been absolutely livid at the mere suggestion that he would ever send a team out to play who would ever give anything less than 100 per cent effort, was that if his gamble in spending what at the time were huge fees to bring in Ian St John and Ron Yeats failed, and Liverpool didn't win promotion, then his rejuvenating of Liverpool may have ended before he had even set the wheels in full motion. Clearly the shareholders were now as impatient for success as Shankly was himself. It's also worth bearing in mind that attendance figures at Anfield had dropped, from an average 38,000 before Shankly arrived, to below the 30,000 mark for the first time since the pre-war years. There was another key factor in the shareholders' concern over Liverpool's continuation as an under-achieving Second Division side. It has been documented that during the early 1960s, Shankly came very close to resigning as Liverpool manager and that it was only his close friend Sir Matt Busby who persuaded him to persevere at Liverpool. It was probably after attending the share-holders' angry annual meeting in 1960 that Shankly came near to terminating his managership of the club. Chairman Williams ended the stormy meeting by reminding them that just a few weeks previously, Scottish international Ian St John had joined the club for a £37,500 fee, and he pledged that *'within the limits of common sense and sound business dealing, the board would do everything possible to bring about the club's return to the First Division'*. Williams concluded by stating: *'When we meet here next year, on the occasion of the seventieth annual meeting, I hope we will have achieved our objective, which unfortunately has eluded us much too long.'*

The signing of Ian St John was to prove crucial to Liverpool's drive towards First Division status. Shankly had been alerted to his possible availability after reading of the player's discontent at Motherwell in the *Sunday Post*. Once given the green light by the board that the money would be made available to sign the talented Scot, Shankly travelled up to see him, with director S.C. Reakes arriving in time to watch St John play for Motherwell against Hamilton Academicals in the Lanarkshire Cup. St John scored and an impressed Reakes was only too happy to open negotiations for his transfer at the end of the game. Newcastle were also interested in him, but after Shankly had worked hard at selling Liverpool to St John, his destination was only ever going to be Anfield. St John quickly became a firm favourite with the Liverpool supporters, and in the mid-1960s the story about the church sign in the city centre that posed the question 'What will you do when Christ comes to lead us again?', which had the response scribbled underneath by one of the Anfield brethren 'Move St John to inside-forward', was retold over and over again.

Shankly's next acquisition during the summer of 1961 was the Dundee United centre half Ron Yeats. Initially Shankly had wanted to bring Jack Charlton from Leeds, but couldn't convince the board that Charlton was worth the money Leeds were asking. Shankly's search for a centre half led him to Yeats and, after initially being rebuffed by Dundee United, Shankly persuaded the Liverpool board to part with £30,000 for the Scot who would prove to be the foundation that much of Liverpool's success in the 1960s would be built on. Interviewed in later years, Yeats said he couldn't resist signing for Shankly after spending just a short period of time in the company of the indomitable Liverpool manager. *'I asked him, "Whereabouts in England is Liverpool?"'* recalled Yeats, meaning where geographically was Liverpool. *'"Oh, we're in the First Division, son" replied Shanks. This took me aback. I said "I thought you were in the Second Division?" Quick as a flash, Shankly replied "When we sign you, we'll be in the First Division next year." How could I fail to sign for someone who had so much faith in me? Shanks was an amazing man, he really was.'*

Shankly himself acknowledged that the arrival of St John and Yeats did more for Liverpool's rise from the Second Division to the First than any other factor. *'Yeats could have played in the Second Division on his own with no other defenders with him and won it'*, Shankly was later to claim. Within months of his arrival, Yeats was appointed team captain, Shankly telling the 6ft 2in Scot, whom he had nicknamed his 'Red Colossus', *'Christ son! You're so big that when you lead the team out, you'll frighten the opposition to death.'*

With Yeats and St John supplementing the squad, Shankly now believed that he had a team that fulfilled the wishes of both the board and the disenchanted Liverpool supporters. With the new season just days away, Shankly told Tom Williams, Eric Sawyer and any other board members that came his way that this Liverpool team would not only win promotion, but also the much coveted FA Cup. He knew that this was make or break time, so he decided to increase the chances of success on the field of play by taking the then-revolutionary step of having their opponents checked on by either himself or a member of staff before every game. He was clearly taking no chances, as another season without promotion would have been a catastrophe. Liverpool's opening game was at Bristol Rovers and resulted in a comfortable 2-0 victory. A few days later, just under 50,000 packed into Anfield to see Liverpool take on the team that many thought would be one of Liverpool's main rivals for promotion, Sunderland. Two goals from Hunt and another from Lewis gave Liverpool another easy win. Leeds and Sunderland away were next on the list and Liverpool knocked in nine more goals to maintain their fantastic start to the season. Liverpool didn't taste their first defeat until mid-October and the promotion that everyone at Anfield had craved for so long looked to be a foregone conclusion. Their attack was knocking in goals for fun, with the Yeats-led defence proving as mean as Shankly had suspected it would be once Yeats was in the line-up. Promotion was clinched on 21 April 1962 against Southampton at Anfield, when a crowd of over 40,000 witnessed their 2-0 victory, both goals coming from Kevin Lewis. Everyone at Anfield was ecstatic – Liverpool had had little to celebrate since the team of Stubbins and company had won the Championship in 1947, and everyone intended to make up for lost time. The players were lost in a sea of celebrating fans as they chanted their heroes' names. The Kop wanted to savour this moment

The jubilant Liverpool team celebrate after clinching promotion to the First Division in 1962 with 2-0 home victory over Southampton. The new hero of the Kop, Ian St John, who missed the game through injury, recalled: *'When the Liverpool fans spotted me on the pitch at the end of the game they hoisted me on to their shoulders. They passed me from one jubilant group to another. I managed to struggle back to the dressing room. My clothes were covered in mud, but I was happy.'*

The Liverpool captain, Ron Yeats, holds the Second Division trophy after being presented with it by the president of the Football League, Joe Richards. From left to right, back row: Paisley, Milne, Furnell, Leishman, Hunt, St John, Callaghan. Front row: Moran, Byrne, A'Court, Yeats, T.V. Wllliams, Joe Richards, Shankly, Melia.

of triumph and wouldn't allow the team to disappear to their dressing room. They refused to leave the ground and chanted 'Liv-er-pool, Liv-er-pool' incessantly. The moment that Shankly had dreamed of since he had moved into football management had arrived. He was leading a football club who were now the size of an army. Right from the start of his managerial career, it was Shankly's aim to harness both the team and the supporters into one. To him, football was a communal experience; the team was an extension of the team on the terraces. Shankly knew from his playing days the type of passion and noise that the Kop and the rest of Anfield was capable of. Now it had reached full fruition and although it frightened even some of the Liverpool players on that momentous spring day in 1962, it would be used to even greater effect to terrify Liverpool's opponents in the years that would follow.

The success of Liverpool added an even greater buzz to a city that was teetering on the brink of musical explosion in the early 1960s. There were also now two First Division teams to be proud of, and buoyed by their team's success, an application was made by Liverpool to the Liverpool City Council to have the city's coat of arms displayed on the players' shirts. They cited the fact that Bolton, Nottingham Forest, Newcastle and other famous clubs had their city's coat of arms displayed on their team shirts. *'Our present badge contains only the Liver Bird'*, stated a representative of the board. *'Surely we could do more for the city of Liverpool by showing the badge abroad and elsewhere in Britain?'* It was all to no avail and Liverpool's request to replace the Liver Bird that would become so symbolic with Liverpool's success in years to come was turned down by the city council.

After winning promotion against Southampton, Liverpool entertained Stoke City at Anfield two days later. A crowd of over 41,000 saw goals by Moran and Jimmy Melia give Liverpool a narrow 2-1 victory over Stoke. The following morning, club secretary James McInnes arrived at Anfield to discover that safe-blowers had forced their way into the club's office and blown open a safe containing all of the previous evening's takings of more than £4,000 and most of the Championship medals that had been deposited there for safe keeping. Liverpool acted quickly in contacting the Football League to obtain replacements for the stolen medals. But the gloss of finally winning promotion had been slightly tarnished by the Anfield intruders.

6

MIND OVER MATTER

Liverpool began the 1962/63 season, their first season in the First Division since 1954, in an unconvincing way. An attendance of 51,000 crammed into Anfield to see them play Lancashire rivals Blackpool, who took the points with a 2-1 victory. An away trip to Manchester City followed by a home game against Blackburn Rovers also failed to see Liverpool register a victory. Shankly put down Liverpool's tentative start to giving too much respect to the opposition. After some hard-hitting team talks, during which Shankly would display his growing expertise in the psychological side of football management, Liverpool's results began to improve. He motivated his team by eulogising about what a wonderful group of players they were and what rubbish most of the so-called First Division elite were. All of Liverpool's opponents came in for the Shankly treatment, particularly the London clubs – Spurs were nicknamed by Shankly 'The Drury Lane fan-dancers' and outstanding Tottenham players such as Dave Mackay, who Shankly had practically begged the Liverpool board to sign when Mackay was still a Hearts player, were branded as over the hill and past it. The idiosyncratic Liverpool boss didn't really believe it, and neither did the majority of his players, but somehow Shankly's rubbishing of the opposition did begin to give his Liverpool players a psychological advantage. Arsenal, West Ham ('a bunch of playboys', including the great Bobby Moore) and every other London club were labelled by Shankly as 'soft southerners'. Practically every First Division team was given the Shankly treatment. Don Revie, who was in the process of creating a Leeds United team that would become Liverpool's major rivals for honours over the next ten seasons, would receive a regular Sunday-morning call from Shankly, who would praise every member of his Liverpool team one by one; no player had a weakness. If Revie managed to get a word in to praise a Leeds player, Shankly would just say *'a fit player, nae bad'*, leaving Revie wondering how his team ever won a game.

Liverpool's results did begin to improve and wins against Manchester City, Sheffield United and West Ham put the team in good heart for the first Merseyside derby for nearly ten years. City rivals Everton were among the favourites to take the League title and were fancied by most neutrals to put one over on Shankly's First Division new boys. There were 73,000 packed into Goodison Park for the eagerly awaited contest, and it was Everton who took first blood with a penalty scored by captain Roy Vernon. Lewis equalised for Liverpool before half-time, followed by another for Everton by Johnny Morrissey in the second half. Most of those present thought the points were in the bag for the blue half of Merseyside. With ninety minutes up on the clock, Liverpool were pressing hard for an equalizer, and winger Alan A'Court dispatched one last cross into the Everton penalty area. Up popped Roger Hunt to evade the challenges of Gordon West and Brian Labone to smack the ball into the Everton net. It was always a feature of Liverpool's play throughout the Shankly years that they fought and fought until the final whistle, and this, like on many other occasions in the future, was one of the games when their philosophy brought its rewards. The Liverpudlians in Goodison erupted as the referee blew for full time within seconds of the Hunt goal that meant so much to their team's standing on Merseyside. Recalling his equaliser years later Hunt remarked: *'The Merseyside derby means so much to so many people. If we had lost, then our supporters would have had to wait six months for a chance of revenge, so to score such an important late goal was an indescribable feeling for me.'*

Jimmy Melia, a key member of the Liverpool team that won the Second Division title in 1962 and the First Division Championship in 1964. Melia represented the Reds 287 times, scoring 78 goals. He was also capped by England during the mid-1960s.

After the game, arguments raged between Everton and Liverpool fans about whether the referee should have blown for time before Hunt's equaliser and should Everton have been awarded a penalty in the first half. But generally, these disagreements were good-natured banter that rarely boiled over into anything physical. Football commentators have remarked many times in the years preceding this first Merseyside derby of the 1960s about the uniqueness of Everton and Liverpool fans walking to the game together and standing (nowadays sitting) side by side during the ninety minutes with little hint of trouble, but this was the first time it had been seen in action by television and the media in general. It was a phenomenon Bill Shankly also found unique and he commented on this during the 1970s: *The rivalry between Everton and Liverpool is like Celtic and*

Bill Shankly, photographed at the beginning of the 1961/62 season. Liverpool finally clinched promotion to the First Division, after several near misses, at the end of this campaign.

Rangers without the bigotry. There are families in Liverpool with two supporting Everton and two supporting Liverpool. I've never seen a fight at a derby game. This is unusual. They are the same people really.'

Despite the confidence booster of the derby draw, Shankly knew that new blood was needed to boost his squad. When he heard that classy Rangers half-back Willie Stevenson was unable to gain a regular first-team place at the Glasgow club, he acted quickly to rescue the Scot from Australian football where he was languishing on loan. A £20,000 fee brought Stevenson to Anfield in October 1962. Photographer Barry Farrell was sent to Anfield to cover the arrival of Stevenson at Liverpool and recalls an incident that displayed how Shankly stamped his mark on a new arrival straight away. *'Negotiations were completed and Shanks was showing Willie around Anfield. One incident sticks in my memory. Shanks stepped out of a car with Willie and they were about to enter the players' entrance. There was a small group of wide-eyed Liverpool kids waiting by the entrance, pens at the ready,*

Gerry Byrne, an outstanding full-back for Liverpool in the 1960s. Byrne felt his Anfield career was going nowhere until Shankly arrived at the club in 1959. Byrne recalled:
'I was beginning to wonder whether I was ever going to make it. I was in the reserves and seriously thinking about leaving when there was a change in manager and Bill Shankly came. Bill had confidence in me and I always tried never to let him down.'

hoping to obtain the autographs of any of their heroes who might happen to pass by. Willie went to walk into the entrance when Shanks exclaimed "Willie, son! You've forgotten something." Liverpool's latest acquisition looked bemused as he wondered what his new boss was talking about. "You've forgotten something, son", Shanks repeated. Willie was still none the wiser. "Willie, son, go and sign the children's books", Shanks quietly ordered. Willie looked relieved and was only too happy to comply with his manager's wishes. It may appear to be an insignificant incident, but it gives an example of how Shankly was eager to display to a new signing that the Anfield brethren, whether young or old, come first.'

Although Stevenson took a little time to settle, once he did he became a key figure in Shankly's team. His passing skills were first class and together with Milne and Jimmy Melia, he became a key member of the Liverpool team that would storm to the League title in such thrilling fashion the following season. Willie was also a joker around the dressing room and helped to create the kind of atmos-

Bill Shankly teaches Ronnie Moran a few tricks of the trade. Moran was a great servant to Liverpool, both as a player and coach, for nearly fifty years.

phere that successful teams thrive under. Shankly also introduced goalkeeper Tommy Lawrence into the team during the same period of Stevenson's introduction and this much-underrated keeper would, like Stevenson, become a key element of Shankly's first great team. The brave Lawrence, who was adept at diving at the feet of opposing forwards bearing in on goal, would also go on to win Scottish international honours. Boosted by the motivational skills of

Shankly and the injection of new blood into the team, Liverpool's results did begin to pick up, and during the November to February period they ran up a sequence of nine consecutive victories. The rest of the First Division now began to realise that Shankly's passionate orations about his outstanding Liverpool team were no longer an idle boast. Liverpool's dramatic improvement in form coincided with one of the worst winters in living memory, with the big freeze leading to the cancellation of many fixtures. It was during the early weeks of January 1963 that most of the country was in the grip of arctic conditions and Shankly was desperate to give his team some much-needed match practice. He contacted Everton manager Harry Catterick and asked him did he fancy taking on his Liverpool team behind closed doors at Everton's training ground at Bellefield. Harry agreed and the game took place on a snow-covered pitch. After the game, which Liverpool lost, Shankly was heard to exclaim, tongue-in-cheek, *'That bloody referee is a disgrace. He shouldn't have allowed that game to take place. The pitch wasn't safe.'*

Although Liverpool couldn't maintain their outstanding League form when League football returned once pitches became playable again, hopes were high that this was going to be the year that they would win the FA Cup for the very first time. After defeating Wrexham 3-0, they were drawn to play Burnley at Turf Moor. At the time, Burnley were a strong First Division outfit and a 1-1 draw in the first game brought the Lancashire side back to Anfield for the replay. A pitch inspection was needed to allow the game to take place. Shankly, vigilant as ever, watched the referee make his way out onto the frosty Anfield turf and then spotted that Burnley manager Harry Potts was also walking out onto the pitch. Shankly had never had much time for the-then Burnley chairman, Bob Lord, an outspoken Lancastrian businessman, and seized on the opportunity to take a swipe at Burnley through their manager Harry Potts. *'Hey you, Potts!'* he shouted to the startled Burnley manager. *'Get off our pitch. You don't find me walking all over your pitch at Turf Moor. Get off it, now!'* The bemused Burnley boss left the referee to make the inspection on his own and the match was given the go-ahead. After extra

Liverpool draw with local rivals Everton at Goodison Park in 1962. Roger Hunt celebrates his last-minute equaliser with Kevin Lewis.

time, Liverpool won the replay and went on to defeat Arsenal and West Ham on their way to a semi-final tie against Leicester. A 65,000 crowd attended the game, held at Hillsborough, but despite continuous pressure, Leicester recorded their third victory over Liverpool that season and Shankly had no doubts that they had had their Wembley dream ended by the best team in the League. Many of the Liverpool team, several of whom would go on to win major honours in the next few seasons, regarded the Leicester defeat as the most disappointing moment of their Anfield career. It was rather odd, in fact, that Shankly would go on to acclaim Leicester as the top team of the season. Leicester were renowned for their defensive capabilities, and a style of play that the attack-minded Shankly would usually have been adverse to in the extreme. But perhaps the fact that 'that lot across the park', Everton, had just been crowned League Champions, playing an attractive style of attacking play that usually would have had Shankly drooling, may have had something to do with his declarations on who were currently the best team in the League.

Although Liverpool's first season back in the First Division ended in disappointing fashion, losing six of their last nine games, including a 7-2 defeat at the hands of 'the Drury Lane fan-dancers' Spurs, Shankly was confident that they could more than hold their own; the new season couldn't come soon enough for the enthusiastic Scot.

7

WE LOVE YOU, YEAH, YEAH, YEAH

Towards the end of the 1962/63 season, Shankly signed a player from his former club, Preston, who would become a crowd-pleaser at Anfield for the rest of the decade. Peter Thompson was what Shankly would describe as a 'twisty-turny' player who reminded the Liverpool boss of the player whom he regarded as 'the star of all the stars', Tom Finney. Together with Ian Callaghan, Thompson would terrorise First Division full-backs in the coming season.

Shankly was supremely optimistic before the beginning of the 1963/64 season and told the Liverpool shareholders that he would bring the Championship to Anfield, and possibly the FA Cup as well. Interviewed by the *Liverpool Echo*, Shankly declared: *'I feel much better now than before the previous two seasons. In one, we started off in the Second Division; in the other we were newly promoted to the First Division. I had some apprehension then; now it has gone. I think we are equal to or better than any other team. If we think along these lines we shall be.'*

He went on to talk about the training methods at Melwood and claimed that the famous 'sweat box', which was a set of boards placed fifteen yards apart into which a player would go and then have to blast the ball from board to board for as long as possible, would give the Liverpool team an edge in fitness over most teams in the League. *'My pet theme is that we shall never get anywhere if we don't work. All our training functions are well thought out. If players think*

Gordon Milne, a classy midfielder who played a key role in Shankly's championship-winning teams of 1964 and 1966. Milne represented Liverpool 277 times and won 14 England caps.

they can add anything to them we will listen.' Asking his players to contribute their opinions on aspects of training and match-play would be a feature of Shankly's tactics during the coming season.

Liverpool actually started their Championship season in disastrous fashion. Although they picked up points away from home, at Anfield they lost their first three games on the trot. Legend has it that Shankly strode into the boardroom after the third defeat and said to the directors *'I can assure you, gentlemen, that we will win a game at Anfield this season!'* and then left the room. On Monday morning, Shankly told all his first-team players to attend a meeting after training. During the post-mortem, he asked every one of his players for their suggestions on why they were failing to show the form they were capable of at Anfield. The general consensus among them was that they were overanxious to do well in front of their home supporters. When the heart-to-heart drew to a close, Shankly knew that he had to work fast to prepare his team for that evening's game

Liverpool prepare to do battle with Everton at Goodison Park during the
1963/64 season. Everton at the time were reigning league champions, but
Liverpool would go on to take their crown at the end of the campaign. Everton
won the derby game 3-1.

Roger Hunt and Ian St John try on their new Gola boots. Hunt and St John were in devastating goalscoring form for Liverpool during the 1963/64 title triumph, Hunt scoring 31 goals and St John 21.

against Wolves. They had beaten the Midlands club 3-1 at Molineux the previous week, but that was away from the white-hot atmosphere at Anfield. Shankly got to work on sending his team out in a more relaxed frame of mind to try to obtain their first home win of the season. The pep talk did the trick and they thrashed Wolves 6-0. But Liverpool's inconsistent start to the new campaign continued the following Saturday when they lost 3-0 away to Sheffield United. The following Saturday, however, Anfield was to witness the victory they had craved since the 1950s – the defeat of arch-rivals and reigning Champions Everton. Close on 52,000 saw two goals from Ian Callaghan, with a late reply from Roy Vernon, win the day for Liverpool. Local hero Callaghan, overjoyed to be the match winner, after the game described his opening goal as a twenty-five-yard 'Bobby Charlton special' that flew past West in the Everton goal. *'As I got the ball, the defence suddenly fell away from me and to my surprise, gave me clear sight of goal. I thought, this is too good to last and so I shot.'* No greater compliment could be paid to the ferocity of Callaghan's piledriver than the *Liverpool Echo*'s correspondent who wrote: *'The shot was as hard as anything Billy Liddell ever delivered. If he plays at Anfield for fifty seasons, Callaghan will never hit one with such power and such lethal direction.'*

The derby victory kick-started Liverpool's season in dramatic style and they went on to win eight of their next nine games. Probably the most crucial of all these victories as Liverpool powered their way to the top of the table was their 1-0 victory against Manchester United at Old Trafford. Ron Yeats scored the goal that won the game, his first for the club. He was beginning to display a quality of play that was more than just that of a stopper centre half. Roger Hunt was also now blossoming into a formidable goalscorer and in one game against Stoke, blasted in 4 goals in thirty-four minutes for goalscoring at its finest. It was during this Christmas

Roger Hunt scores against Spurs at White Hart Lane, 1964.

fixture against Stoke which Liverpool went on to win 6-1, that the Kop took to singing Beatles songs to display their pride; not only just in their heroes in red shirts on the pitch, but also the pride they felt in watching their fellow Scousers, John, Paul, Gorge and Ringo take the pop world by storm. As thousands of Koppites sang 'We love you, Yeah! Yeah! Yeah! over and over again, Boxing Day at Anfield in 1963 was a fabulous place to be.

A few weeks later, Anfield was treated to another goals bonanza as Liverpool thrashed Sheffield United 6-1, Kop idol Ian St John grabbing a hat-trick. It was Willie Stevenson, however, whom the *Liverpool Echo* voted their man of the match: '*He varies his production of the ball, he can angle a short telling pass or punch one down the centre with the artistry one only associates with wing halves of top class.*'

It was during the Easter period that Liverpool really emerged as Championship contenders. On Good Friday, Hunt scored a hat-trick against Spurs at White Hart Lane to give them a 3-1 victory. The following day, Liverpool travelled to Leicester to take on their bogey team. Another 3-1 win put Liverpool in great heart for their Easter Monday clash with Spurs back at Anfield. Two goals from St John and one from Alf Arrowsmith, who was proving himself somewhat of a sensation after the injury to midfield general Jimmy Melia prompted Shankly to move St John into a deeper role with Arrowsmith and Roger Hunt up front, gave Liverpool a comfortable victory. Bill Shankly was later to claim that playing St John at midfield and introducing Arrowsmith in to the team were important factors in Liverpool's Championship victory. Liverpool's next game was against their Championship rivals Manchester United and Alf Arrowsmith once again displayed his considerable promise, scoring two, with Callaghan adding another as Liverpool ran out comfortable 3-0 winners. It appeared that even the combined talents of Charlton, Law and Best couldn't stop the red machine from powering their way to the title.

Liverpool clinched the First Division Championship, fittingly at Anfield against Arsenal. This time it was wing maestro Peter Thompson who scored a brace, with further goals from St John,

The triumphant Liverpool team go on a lap of honour after clinching the First Division title with a 5-0 thrashing of Arsenal. Ian St John, recalling the game, said: *'It was another of those never to be forgotten afternoons at Anfield. The Kop choir was singing long before the game started. Arsenal never looked like making a game of it. To be fair, we would have thrashed any team in the world that day. No one could stop us.'*

Arrowsmith and Hunt allowing Liverpool to demolish the London team 5-0. Shankly's prophecy that the title would come to Anfield had come true. The acclamation that the new Champions received was even more euphoric than the reception Liverpool were given when they won promotion two years earlier. The Kop serenaded the crestfallen Arsenal team as they waited for the final whistle to end their misery with a rendition of *London Bridge Is Falling Down*. After they had departed the scene, the Kop choir went into full swing, hailing their heroes with chant after chant of 'Liverpool, Liverpool'. The team paraded around Anfield with a home-made replica of the Championship trophy that a fan had handed to captain Ron Yeats, the real thing still taking pride of place in the trophy room across

Stanley Park at Everton. Rumours were that Everton had refused to hand over the trophy. One local reporter, despatched to Anfield to cover the game, admitted that he was even more captivated by the occasion as a whole: *'I've never seen anything to match this in all the years I've been attending. It was the Anfield crowd's day. There have been occasions in the past when one has been almost ashamed to say one came from "Liverpule". This behaviour at a match which had everything at stake made one proud to be remotely associated with a city finding fame afresh for its standards of football and now for crowd behaviour. From an hour before kick-off until nearly three hours later, this was a Liverpool crowd at its Sunday best.'*

The fact that the BBC not only sent camera crews to cover the game, but also for a feature on the Kop to be shown in Monday evening's *Panorama* current affairs programme, gives one an idea of the national interest that was being shown in the phenomenon that the Anfield supporters had now become. Football fans had sung before at games, but not with the passion, humour and spontaneity of the Kop. Social anthropologists pondered over who organised it all – did they practice in the pub before the game? Did someone hand out sheets with chants and songs printed on them? The answer was that it was all spontaneous. It began with chants in homage to their favourite players and after the advent of the Beatles and other Merseybeat bands such as Gerry and the Pacemakers, they decided to change the words slightly, thus *She Loves You* became 'We Love You'. Other Kop favourites of the time such as *'Ee-Aye-Addio'* could be traced back to songs and chants sung by Liverpool children in street games. When watching fans at other clubs witnessed the singing and chanting of the Kop on *Match of the Day* it was inevitable that they would imitate this at their own grounds. Few, however, were ever able to match the sheer inventiveness of the Liverpool fans of the 1960s. It was a phenomenon that will probably never be witnessed again, not even at Anfield.

With the Championship safely won, Shankly, who normally drilled into his players that every game had to be treated like a cup final, with maximum effort for the full ninety minutes, relaxed a

Bill Shankly took his victorious title-winning team to America at the end of the 1963/64 season. After the sensational first U.S. tour by the Beatles, Americans wanted to meet anyone with Liverpool connections, and here the Reds can be seen on *The Ed Sullivan Show*. Shankly didn't enjoy the tour and refused to appear on the show.

little and displayed a more facetious side to his character. He took goalkeeper Tommy Lawrence to one side during training and told him, *'Tom, wouldn't it be great if we could put a deckchair in the middle of the goal, you sitting in it, cigar in your mouth, and when the ball comes, you get out of your deckchair and catch it and say, "It's a lovely day to play football, isn't it?"'* Tommy decided not to put into practice his boss's idea, but Liverpool did ease up a little, losing two of their final three games.

8

SHANKLY'S RED ARMY
AT WEMBLEY

When Liverpool reported back for preseason training at the beginning of the 1964/65 season, Shankly and his squad were greeted with shock news. Key player Ian St John was recovering in a local hospital after a rushed appendix operation. The cause of the problem was the stone from a date that Ian had eaten during the Christmas period. Ian showed his visitor the full-sized stone, which he had been given by the medical staff as a memento of his operation. Although Shankly was renowned for ignoring injuries to his players unless they were chronic, this was one occasion when he had to accept that one of the vital cogs in his Liverpool team wouldn't be available until well into the season. Nevertheless, Shankly and his players were in high spirits. They had their first-ever adventures into Europe to look forward to and they were confident that they could build on the success of the previous campaign. They also had a new chairman, Sidney Reakes, who had taken over from T. V. Williams, who was now club president. Williams had decided to make way for a younger man but was keen to point out that he would still do all he could to assist the club and players. Speaking to his local paper, he suggested that the success of Liverpool would soon result in bigger pay packets for the team: *'If they put up good performances, they will get good gates, and if they get good gates, they will get something for the kitty and their days of retirement.'* But within a year, there would be upheaval over financial

The Liverpool team parade the First Division trophy before the start of the 1964/65 season. From left to right, back row: Milne, Byrne, Lawrence, Moran, Stevenson, Paisley. Front row: Bennett, Callaghan, Hunt, T.V. Williams (chairman), Yeats, Arrowsmith, Thompson, Shankly.

rewards at Anfield. Bill Shankly, never one to dwell over money matters, concerned himself only with the coming season. He told his team: *'I said this time last year that a fit Liverpool who fought hard were capable of beating anyone. This you bore out by lifting the Championship of England, which is really the Championship of Great Britain. We have simple training methods and a simple, but positive way of playing. If you carry it out with the same dedication you'll win the title again.'*

He then went on to talk to the press who were curious about Liverpool's training methods. *'It's simple'*, he claimed. *'The system is based on exhaustion and recovery, building up players' stamina to enable them to produce their inherent skill and footballing ability, despite the speed of the game, from the first minute to the ninetieth.'* Although the press accepted Shankly's explanation of his training formula, there was still the nagging feeling that the Liverpool boss was holding back on a secret training formula that gave his team the edge over most others. Within football, the secrets of Liverpool's success would grow into mythical proportions with the coming years, but Shankly was revealing all; the Liverpool secret of success was based predominantly on simplicity and hard work.

Willie Stevenson, a fantastic signing by Shankly from Rangers for just £20,000 in 1962. Stevenson was outstanding in Liverpool's title triumphs in 1964 and 1966. He played 237 times for the Reds. Stevenson, like most of the Shankly players, has nothing but fond memories of the great man. He said: *'I remember Bill Shankly most for his sense of humour. He was also a very fair man and nowhere near as hard as people liked to make him out to be. All he wanted was dedication and every man to play for his teammates. I consider myself fortunate to have played under him.'*

As with everything that took place at Anfield, Shankly's preparation for the coming campaign left nothing to chance. The players' level of fitness would gradually be built up, with the risk of strains and pulled muscles kept to a minimum. Practice games would begin initially on a full-size pitch, before progressing to just half the playing area. Eventually, with a higher level of fitness now achieved, the players would play five-a-side in a quarter of the pitch to allow them to sharpen up their first touch and distribution; the confined area of play allowing no time to dwell on the ball.

Liverpool's opening game of the season was actually the away tie in the opening round of the European Cup. They were due to play Icelandic Champions Reykjavik and Shankly was determined that their first European adventure would be something to remember.

Ron Yeats still chuckles when he recalls their trip to Iceland. *'It was unbelievable. We travelled from Liverpool to Manchester, Manchester to London and then Shanks decided that when we touched down at Prestwick, he would show us around Ayrshire, where he came from, before the final flight to Iceland. He then had a coach waiting for us in Scotland to take us to a Butlin's Holiday Camp. We all trooped on to the coach and when we arrived at Butlin's, Shanks introduced himself to the fellow on the door: "Bill Shankly, manager of Liverpool Football Club en route to Iceland to play in the European Cup." The man on the door shook his head and said, "I think you've taken the wrong road sir!" I can't say what Shanks said to the fellow, but we were all marched back on to the coach. We were bursting to laugh, but daren't.'* Liverpool won the tie easily 11-1 over the two legs, and were drawn to meet the formidable Belgian Champions Anderlecht in the next round.

Liverpool's only new signing to strengthen the squad for the coming season was the Manchester United forward Phil Chisnall, with Arsenal's Geoff Strong joining later in the season. Liverpool's opening league game of the season was against the team they had thrashed just a few months earlier to clinch the title, Arsenal. This time the Londoners made Liverpool fight all the way for a 3-2 victory, two of the Liverpool goals coming from Gordon Wallace who was deputising for the recuperating Ian St John. This game was also chosen by the BBC for their inaugural *Match of the Day* programme. As with the previous season, however, Liverpool didn't start the new campaign too convincingly. The absence of St John hit

Bill Shankly chats to the press at Melwood, 1965.

the team severely, and Liverpool were also unfortunate to be without Alf Arrowsmith, who had sustained a bad knee injury in a Charity Shield game against West Ham. Liverpool lost five of their first eight games and it looked as though retaining the Championship was slipping out of their reach. Shankly introduced nineteen-year-old Bobby Graham into the team for the home game against Aston Villa, and the young Scot was an immediate sensation, scoring a hat-trick in Liverpool's 5-1 victory. Graham scored again when Liverpool defeated Sheffield United 3-1 in their next game, but in general, their League form during the 1964/65 season was disappointing and inconsistent. The signing of Geoff Strong, whom Shankly converted into one of the most efficient utility players in England, and the emergence of Liverpool teenager Tommy Smith added much-needed depth to the squad, but it was to be only in the cup competitions that Liverpool would shine this season. Tommy Smith had actually made his Liverpool debut at home to Birmingham in May 1963, but had to wait until August of 1964 for his next first-team League outing. Shankly recalled that Smith grew so impatient waiting for another chance that he decided to take matters into his own hands. Shankly said: *'He was always knocking on the door to ask when he was going to get a first-team chance. One day we were playing five-a-side and Tommy slid into Chris Lawler and caught him on the ankle. Chris's ankle went up like a balloon. We were all disturbed about Chris. As we were coming off the training ground, Tommy said to me, "Will I be in the team on Saturday?" He'd just crippled Chris and then wanted to know would he be in the team. He was.'* Once he was established in the Liverpool team, Tommy Smith became a permanent and vital cog in the Shankly team that would achieve so much success over the next two seasons. Although renowned for his hard tackling, Smith had much more to his game than that. *'You don't play over 600 times for Liverpool under great managers like Shankly and Paisley, if all you can do is kick people'*, he once angrily proclaimed; and he was right.

Although struggling in the League, Liverpool were enjoying their first venture into Europe. Belgian Champions Anderlecht would provide far stiffer opposition than Liverpool's first-round victims Reykjavik, but the Shankly team managed to come through the tie without too much difficulty. It was prior to the home leg that Shankly, always on the lookout for a psychological advantage over his opponents, decided to change the Liverpool strip to all red for the first time. He told Ron Yeats to put on the new strip and run out of the tunnel. Shankly stood on the pitch and couldn't hide his glee: *'Jesus Christ, son, you look bloody massive. You'll scare them to death!'* The all-red strip that became Liverpool's trademark, was here to stay. *'It'll make the team look even tougher, bigger and more formidable to the opposition'*, Shankly told the press and when one thinks about it, it actually did.

After giving his team a pre-match pep talk, the gist of it being that the Belgian team were rubbish and should feel privileged to be playing Liverpool, the home team went out and won 3-0. After the game, an animated Shankly told his team: *'Christ, boys, you've just beaten one of the finest teams in Europe!'* The return leg in Belgium was due to take place just before the Christmas holiday period on 16 December but the journey wasn't without incident. The Viscount airliner that was due to fly the team to Belgium was at the centre of an emergency alert at Liverpool airport. As Shankly and his team waited in the terminal building for the aircraft to arrive, the captain of the Viscount contacted air traffic control to relay the news to them that smoke was entering the flight deck. Emergency services and fire engines stood by as the stricken plane touched down at Liverpool. Thankfully, the aircraft was brought safely to ground and the fire was traced to a short-circuit in the electric system. Eventually, the twenty-four-strong Liverpool party set off safely on their way to Belgium, but it was incidents such as that which led to Shankly always being the most reluctant of travellers. A Roger Hunt goal gave Liverpool a 1-0 victory in front of 60,000 frustrated Anderlecht supporters. The rest of Europe was beginning to take notice of an emerging red threat from Liverpool.

Liverpool's League form had also now become more consistent and they remained unbeaten from November 1964 through to

Left: A pitch inspection at Anfield before the European Cup tie against Cologne, 1965.

Below: Ian St John in action against Cologne in the European Cup 1965. After three gruelling games failed to provide a winner, Liverpool won the tie on the toss of a coin.

27 February 1965. Victories over West Brom and Stockport in the cup also pleased Shankly, who knew that the prize that every Liverpudlian wanted above all others was the FA Cup.

The draw for the next round of the European Cup paired Liverpool with German club FC Cologne. The first leg took place in Cologne and it turned out to be quite a trip for Liverpool, with the Mayor of Liverpool and a delegation of civic dignitaries travelling to Germany to support the Reds, using the occasion to cement the long-standing friendship between the two cities. Lord Mayor Alderman Louis Caplan said: '*I met the burgomaster last summer and I know he is a keen supporter of Cologne, so I hope to prepare the way for a civic delegation from Cologne to come back to Liverpool for the return match.*' The Liverpool players returned home, quietly satisfied with themselves after a hard-fought 0-0 draw. The return leg at Anfield, however, proved equally as tough and once again, there was no score. A third game was arranged at a neutral venue, which turned out to be Rotterdam, and once again the match finished all square at 2-2. The outcome now had to be decided on the toss of a coin. It was a nerve-racking moment for Shankly and his team as captain Ron Yeats stepped up with the Cologne captain to decide who would go through to the European Cup semi-finals. Ron Yeats recalled: '*When it came to the toss of the coin, I thought "get in quick". I said, "I'll have tails, referee" and the referee said, "Okay, Liverpool tails, Cologne heads." When he tossed it, I couldn't believe it. It stuck in a divot on its side. The referee picked up the coin and tossed it again. It came down tails. I could see Shanks at the side of the pitch. He said to me as I walked off, "Well done, big man, what did you pick?" I said tails. "I would have picked that myself", said Shanks and he just walked away. I was waiting for the adulation, but he just walked away.*' With a place in the European Cup semi-finals now in the bag, Liverpool turned their attention back to domestic matters. Just three days after their energy-sapping exploits in the European Cup, Liverpool were due to meet Chelsea in the FA Cup semi-final at Villa Park. Liverpool had disposed of bogey team Leicester City in the quarter-finals after a replay and were now confident that this would finally be the year that the FA

Chris Lawler, a fabulous full-back for Liverpool during the Shankly era. Lawler was dubbed 'The Silent Knight' by the Kop because of his unassuming, modest nature. He would ghost into goalscoring positions unnoticed by the opposition and scored numerous important goals for the club. Lawler made 546 appearances for the Reds, scoring 61 goals, an incredible tally for a full-back. Lawler said of the 1960s Liverpool team: *'There was a great team spirit. We were all on the same basic wage, £45 per week. We were all on the same bonuses and there were no arguments in the dressing-room.'*

Cup would come to Anfield. Tommy Docherty's Chelsea were only too pleased to watch Liverpool struggle to overcome Cologne on television just a few days prior to the semi, and were confident that they would take advantage of an exhausted Liverpool team. Bill Shankly had always proclaimed to anyone who would listen that his team were by far the fittest group of players in Britain and in the semi-final Liverpool proved this was no idle boast. Chelsea did match Liverpool until just after the hour mark, but then Peter Thompson struck and Wembley was within their sights. Willie Stevenson added another from the penalty spot and the game was won. Shankly's lifelong friend, Tommy Docherty, admitted that Chelsea were beaten by a superior team on the day. Liverpool's opponents at Wembley were to be Don Revie's Leeds United; a team that were as hard, as fit, but, for the time being, not yet as talented as Shankly's Liverpool. Winning the FA Cup for the first time in their history wouldn't be easy for Ron Yeats and company.

Once Liverpool had booked their Wembley place, Merseyside went into a football frenzy; particularly when it came to the pursuit of the ever elusive cup final ticket. Liverpool fans' expectations were high that they would deliver the Cup back to Anfield, and they all wanted to be at Wembley to witness the historic event. Liverpool's

Above: Two great managers of the 1960s and early 1970s, Don Revie of Leeds and Bill Shankly of Liverpool, lead out their teams before the start of the 1965 FA Cup final. With his motivational skills to the fore, Shankly sent out his side with the following team talk: *'Leeds are honoured and lucky to be on the same pitch as you. You will win because you are fitter, harder and more skilled. You will win because you must not disappoint the finest supporters in the world. If necessary, you should be prepared to die for them.'*

Below: The 1965 FA Cup final between Liverpool and Leeds was played out on a rainy day at Wembley. The Liverpool and Leeds benches can be seen here doing their best to shelter from the rain. The tenseness of the game is etched into their faces.

Geoff Strong lets fly at the Leeds goal during the 1965 FA Cup final.

average gate at Anfield during the 1964/65 season was over 41,000, but Liverpool's Wembley allocation was only 15,000 tickets. Liverpool were inundated with phone calls and begging letters from fans desperate for tickets. Bill Shankly attempted to obtain as many tickets as he could to supply the fans who supported the team week in and week out. *'Any tickets I've got are going to the boys on the Kop'*, he angrily told one caller from Birmingham who claimed that he'd been a Liverpool fan all his life. Liverpool chairman Sidney Reakes received a phone call from Leeds United Supporters Club requesting a ticket, as a gesture of goodwill between the clubs, for the newly crowned beauty queen Miss Leeds United. Apparently Leeds had turned down this request themselves, so the supporters club decided to try Liverpool.

With the cup final approaching Liverpool did ease off in the League, using the remaining weeks of the season to rest some of the first-teamers and allow others time to recover from injuries. The unlucky Gordon Milne was trying desperately to get himself fit for the final, but was destined not to recover in time. Interviewed a few days before the final, Bill Shankly told the *Liverpool Echo* that he had personally watched Leeds three times during the past two weeks and

The Leeds goalkeeper Gary Sprake and defender Jack Charlton defend against another Liverpool attack.

considered that they were at their most dangerous at set pieces. When the questioning turned to tickets, Shankly told the *Echo*, *'Correspondence has become mountainous since we reached the final. There are pleas for tickets in every post from people I haven't seen or heard of for years. It's simply impossible to help them.'*

When the day of the final arrived Shankly had his team well prepared. Unfortunately, Gordon Milne's knee injury kept him out, but the other doubt, Ian Callaghan, was declared fit to play, although only after continuous treatment. During the train journey to London, in fact, Bob Paisley sat with Callaghan in the guard's van continuing applying iced-water compresses to the Liverpool winger's leg until the train arrived in the capital. Paisley's dedicated treatment did the trick for Callaghan, with his perpetual running, was a deciding factor in Liverpool's success. After missing out in the League to Manchester United on goal averages, Leeds were just as desperate to win the Cup as Liverpool. A classic battle of the roses was anticipated, but, as so often happens in Cup finals, tension of the occasion affected both teams, and neither played to their full potential. Liverpool's hopes took a blow early in the game when full-back Gerry Byrne was on the receiving end of a crunching

Above: An extra-time winner from Ian St John won the FA Cup for the first time in Liverpool's history in 1965. Ron Yeats and St John hold the cup aloft with their teammates after their famous victory. St John said after the game: *'After I scored the winning goal, the last nine minutes seemed like a lifetime. We were thinking, "let's just hang on". I don't ever remember going up for the cup.'*

challenge from the diminutive but hard-as-iron Leeds captain Bobby Collins. Byrne sustained a broken collarbone in the collision, but managed to keep the extent of his injury from the Leeds camp, and even Shankly himself refused to believe Bob Paisley when he told the Liverpool boss that the full-back's collarbone was fractured. Byrne was obviously in extreme pain but the heroic full-back played out not only the whole game, but extra time as well. Substitutes hadn't yet been introduced into the British game, so for a ten-man Liverpool to have beaten a formidable Leeds team would have been highly unlikely. After a dour ninety minutes, the game ended in stalemate. The deadlock was finally broken three minutes into extra time, when Byrne sent in a cross for Roger Hunt to open the scoring. The Liverpool contingent at Wembley went berserk. *'Ee-aye-addio, we've won the Cup'* rang around the stadium. Just eight minutes later their singing came to sudden halt as Billy Bremner, a player who never stopped trying until the game was over, struck an equaliser for Leeds. Liverpool were stunned. With just nine minutes remaining of the second period of extra time, Liverpool's Mr Perpetual Motion, Ian Callaghan, fired in a cross for Ian St John to fling himself forward and bullet the ball past Gary Sprake. A crest-fallen Leeds didn't recover from this blow and the FA Cup was Liverpool's. Wembley had never witnessed celebrations like it, as Ron Yeats stepped up to take the trophy. It was a mixture of euphoria and relief that the Liverpudlians felt as they stood and cheered their team as they paraded around Wembley. No longer would Evertonians be able to sneer at them as they posed the question 'When are Liverpool going to win the Cup?' The cup was now theirs; Shankly, their messiah, had delivered the goods yet again. As the rest of the nation watched on television as the joyous scenes unfolded, they now knew that the men from Anfield had fully

Ron Yeats holds the FA Cup in 1965, flanked by Tommy Lawrence and Geoff Strong. Billy Bremner, said after the game: *Liverpool were a magnificent side. Bill Shankly transformed them into a very special outfit. He was a canny guy and everyone respected him.'*

arrived as a soccer force. In later years, Shankly spoke of the satisfaction that winning the Cup brought him: *'I thought it was a terrible disgrace that Liverpool had had to suffer the taunts for seventy-three years that they hadn't won the FA Cup. Never mind winning the European Cup; winning the FA Cup was the hardest thing.'* The reception that greeted the triumphant Liverpool team when they arrived back in the city for their homecoming hadn't been witnessed since the days of Dixie Dean and his Everton team parading around Liverpool with the Cup in 1933.

Bill Shankly's wife, Nessie, who very rarely attended football matches, was at Wembley in 1965 and still has vivid memories of the homecoming: *'We arrived at Lime Street station and I'd never seen such crowds. They were ecstatic. That really was our first experience of the Liverpool people proper. Bill was over the moon, as we all were.'* It was estimated that over 250,000 lined the city centre streets as the Liverpool coach drove towards the town hall. To Shankly, the real

Opposite: Liverpool parade the FA Cup through the streets of Liverpool, 1965. Ian St John, whose winning goal won the day for the Reds, said: *'200,000 turned out to cheer us from Lime Street to the town hall for a civic reception. The acting Chief Constable said it was the biggest crowd that the city had ever seen. Bigger than when Everton won the cup in 1933. Bigger even than for the Beatles' reception a year before ours.'*

Left: Bill Shankly salutes the fans at Wembley in 1965 after Liverpool's extra-time victory. He told his team before the extra-time period: *'Leeds have shot their bolt. They have had it. Go right in for the kill.'*

joy of winning was in sharing his and his team's happiness with the
multitudes who supported them, and in witnessing the joy
Liverpool's victory had brought to the people of the city. It was
almost as if he was more pleased for them than for himself. Roger
Hunt, reflecting on Liverpool's FA Cup victory in 1965, recently
commented: *'The fantastic enthusiasm of those fans underlined to me
that playing a part in bringing the Cup back to Anfield ranked as my
greatest achievement at the time. Even in the light of what happened after-
wards* [England's World Cup victory in 1966], *I'm not sure that I ever
topped it.'*

Watching Liverpool's Wembley victory with interest at their Southport headquarters were Inter Milan manager Helenion Herrera and his team. Just three days after their Cup victory, Liverpool were due to meet Inter in the first leg of the European Cup semi-final. Herrera was suitably impressed and told the press that he expected a very hard match. The Inter manager was probably quietly confident that his team would be able to contain the new English Cup holders without too much difficulty. He knew all about the energy-sapping Wembley turf, and with extra time being played as well, Liverpool were bound to be a little leg weary. The Liverpool that he saw against Leeds was also not Shankly's team at their best. On the evening of the game, Anfield was packed nearly two hours before kick-off time. Ron Yeats remembered arriving at an almost eerie ground with few people in the outlying street: *'We didn't realize everyone was inside the ground. The police had actually requested that Liverpool open the turnstiles at 3.30 to ease the congestion in the streets and by 5.30, the gates of the Kop were closed.'*

Shankly, as ever relentless in his pursuit of a psychological advantage over the opposition, decided to send Wembley hero Gerry Byrne and Liverpool's other injured star, Gordon Milne, out early to parade the FA Cup in front of the fans. Shankly's ploy did the trick and the duo received a tremendous reception. Apparently, the Kop had been singing prior to this gesture *'Ee-aye-addio, we wanna see the Cup.'* Shankly heard this and decided to comply with the Kop's wishes. The Inter team were actually out on the pitch warming up when Byrne and Milne emerged with it. Although the Italians were experienced European campaigners, the roar of the Kop must have unsettled them. Shankly didn't really need to give his team a pep talk. Tommy Smith says that Shankly said very little: *'Shanks never put any fear into us. He just said get out there and enjoy it. We'd won the FA Cup. We went out and showed the Italians how to play. We murdered them.'* Ron Yeats recollects *'Anfield was buzzing, absolutely buzzing. There was steam coming from the Kop. The hair still stands up on the back of my neck when I talk about the Milan game.'* It's often claimed that football teams are shaped in the image of their manager. Shankly was once quoted as saying *'My idea was to build Liverpool into a bastion of invincibility. My idea was to conquer the bloody world; and be untouchable. Everyone would have to submit and give in.'*

Liverpool's performance against the reigning European Champions Inter Milan at Anfield that evening in May 1965 epitomised Shankly's ideals for his team. Roared on by the Kop chant of 'Attack, Attack, Attack', Liverpool tore into Inter and knocked them totally out of their stride. Roger Hunt opened the scoring after only four minutes, pouncing on a Callaghan cross to swivel and smash the ball into the net. The brilliant Italians hit back almost immediately with Mazzola netting after a sweet Inter move. Liverpool kept to their task and Callaghan put them back into the lead after thirty-four minutes. For the rest of the game, Liverpool bombarded the Inter goal and were unfortunate to only score one more goal, a St John effort, to take back to Milan. To beat the European Cup holders 3-1 was still, however, a magnificent effort by the Anfield team. The game has now reached almost legendary status, and to Ian St John it was a milestone in the rise of Shankly's team: *'The cup final at Wembley drained everybody. To take on the might of Inter Milan was the "night of nights". There have been many great nights at Anfield, but I think when people look back, they will say that was the night when Liverpool really came of age.'*

Liverpool's demolition of Inter was greeted with a mixture of surprise and acclaim by both the English and Italian press. Many Italian papers admitted that Inter had been lucky to escape with only a 3-1 defeat. One Milan daily wrote: *'Inter were dazed. We lift off our hats to Liverpool. They are a marvellous team.'* Another said *'On the field, Liverpool found all the energies which we thought would be lost after their exhausting battle for the FA Cup. The moving, colourful, picturesque and electrifying support of their fans is not enough to explain the surprising technical quality of their game. The breath of the man who shouts, does not help the man who has to run. It was a miracle, a triumph of athletic soccer; soccer played to win; soccer in which all energies were aimed at the adversary's goal. When a team which understands football in this way wins, the inevitable bitterness of defeat for the Italians is lessened. Soccer played this way belongs to all, everyone would like to see it played this way. For the first time, our World Champions felt the earth tremble under their feet and were unable to find sufficient force to react.'*

The return leg in Milan a week later is a game that over thirty years later still arouses anger in the Liverpool players who participated. The atmosphere at Anfield may have been hysterical, but it was nothing to the din that greeted Liverpool when they stepped out onto the San Siro pitch to take in the surroundings before the game began. Ron Yeats claims it was one of Shankly's few mistakes during his managership of Liverpool: *'I think it was one time when Bill slipped up. He took us out on to the pitch and the atmosphere was electric. They were shooting rockets; not into the sky, but down at us on the pitch. It really was frightening.'* Bill Shankly summed it up in a few words: *'It was a war; I've never seen such hostility.'*

When Liverpool ran out to face Inter, 90,000 hostile fans greeted them with deafening klaxon horns, smoke bombs and rockets. They were up against it from the world go. Inter Milan were without any shadow of doubt an excellent team and may well have won the tie through playing the excellent football they were capable of, but a series of controversial refereeing decisions went in Inter's favour. Liverpool's game plan was to soak up early Inter pressure and hit them on the break. This was in tatters after only ten minutes when they found themselves two goals down, both goals a result of highly debatable refereeing decisions. The first was scored by Corso directly from a free kick that should have been awarded as an indirect. The second was scored by Peiro, who kicked the ball from Tommy Lawrence's hands as he bounced the ball and tapped it into the Liverpool net. The Liverpool players were furious, but the referee waved away all protests and Liverpool were now under considerable pressure not only to stop Inter scoring a third, but to keep their heads over the referee's dubious decisions. With Inter striving for the goal that would take them to the final, the San Siro was now a cauldron of noise. Inter's European experience was now very much in evidence and after relentless pressure Facchetti scored the winner. As the Liverpool team trooped wearily off the pitch at the end of

Tommy Lawrence is left sprawling on the turf after Inter Milan scored against Liverpool in the European Cup semi-final second leg, 1965. Inter won 3-0 and went through to the final 3-2 on aggregate.

the game, Tommy Smith admits that he actually assaulted the referee: *'That referee is on my hit list. I've never come across him since but I'll admit that as we came off the pitch in Milan, I kicked him. I just booted him and he never changed his step, or even registered that I kicked him. He just kept on walking and I thought, "Yeah, you have been fiddled". Because at the end of the day, he actually should have sent me off, or done something about it. If somebody kicked, I'd give them a clip back.'* Bill Shankly was furious about the refereeing of the game but refused to lodge a protest. *'Above all things in continental football, you expect to get protection for the goalkeeper. The referee never protected Lawrence in this case and Peiro kicked him on the arm to get possession of the ball. The goal was a disgrace.'*

The Italian newspapers were delighted that Inter had reached the European Cup final, but still found time to praise Liverpool. One Milan paper declared: *'Milan has won the most difficult game of its history through a gigantic performance of its defence. Certainly it must have been a torment to play and lose thus, in front of such a public – which undoubtedly surpassed even the madmen of Liverpool.'* The public of

Milan went wild that night with Inter fans driving around the city streets waving flags from their cars. One Liverpool fan told the *Liverpool Echo*: *'We couldn't understand what they were saying but crowds of Inter fans were trying to take the mickey. It was peaceful enough, however; no punch-ups followed the game.'*

Shankly's dream of leading Liverpool to a unique Cup double was now over, but he had seen nothing in Europe that concerned him. He said: *'In the European Cup you meet cunning, bluff and gimmicks. So much of the continental game is based on the safety-first principle, to the detriment of entertainment.'* He wanted to win every game by making the opposition 'submit and give in' but he wouldn't win a European trophy until he reassessed his all-out attack approach in the early 1970s.

9

THE BEST TEAM IN ENGLAND SINCE THE WAR

Liverpool reported for preseason training at the beginning of the 1965/66 season locked in dispute over their request for an increased wage deal. Liverpool's basic wage during the 1960s was among the lowest levels in the First Division. Win bonuses and other bonuses based on attendance figures increased their salary, but as FA Cup winners and European Cup semi-finalists, they considered that they had a good case for an increase in their basic wage. A key Liverpool player in the team once remarked *'If you didn't win you didn't eat.'* Ian St John openly admits that the top basic wage he ever received during his ten-year spell at Liverpool was £40 a week. That was in 1971, just before he left the club. Bill Shankly didn't like to talk money with his players. He was always content with a decent basic wage throughout his career as a player and he thought his players should have the same attitude to the game. Former Liverpool manager Roy Evans once asked Shankly if his wages could be increased to £30 a week, and although the Liverpool boss was sympathetic to Evans' request, he still left Shankly's office without his wages increased. A fringe Liverpool player of the 1960s made an impassioned plea to Shankly to increase his wages because his father had recently died and his family was finding it hard to manage. Shankly asked the player if anyone else in his family was working. The Liverpool reserve told his boss that his sister also had a job. *'Tell*

The Liverpool team before the start of the 1965/66 season. From left to right, back row: Milne, Byrne, Lawrence, Yeats, Lawler, Stevenson. Front row: Callaghan, Hunt, St John, Smith, Thompson.

her to ask her boss for a rise then, you'll not be getting any more money here', was Shankly's response.

What appears to be a very hard-hearted attitude to his players' requests for better wages is hard to understand. Shankly was the man who on many occasions would take out his wallet and hand over significant sums of money to Liverpool fans who might be stranded far away from home after supporting the team. He would also give financial assistance to Liverpool supporters who were finding it difficult to pay their rent. The Liverpool boss also visited numerous terminally-ill children and their families for days on end helping to get them through probably the most difficult time they would face in their lives. Shankly did all of this and much more for people who were in need of his help. But when it came to wages, he could be tough. In later years when Tommy Smith was team captain, he asked him to get the rest of the players together and see what the feelings were about a new wage structure. *'You sort it out for me, Tommy'*, said Shankly. *'I'll call back later and see what you come up with.'* And with that the Liverpool boss left Smith to it. Later that day Shankly returned to find out his players' feelings. Tommy Smith remembers what happened next: *'The players came up with one or two little things. When Shanks came up to me, I told him I'd had a word with the lads and this is what we suggest. He looked at the list and after each suggestion he said "No! No! No! son!" He then turned to me and said, "Do yer know what, Smithy, you could cause a riot in a graveyard." He then began to argue with me. I couldn't believe it.'* Ian St John claims that Shankly and his great friend at Manchester United, Sir Matt Busby, both of whom came from a very poor mining background in Scotland, were worried about their players getting involved in spiralling wage increases and that the two of them colluded to keep wages down.

Peter Thompson, followed by Chris Lawler, take the field of play for Liverpool in 1965. Thompson loved his days at Liverpool under Bill Shankly but he never failed to be surprised by his idiosyncratic manager. He recalled: *'You could go for sixty games without injury, but if you missed one, Shankly would call you a hypochondriac, and be deadly serious. Another time, Bob Paisley came up to me after training and told me Shankly wanted to see me. I was a bit worried, and Bill looked very serious. "I'm disappointed in you, Thommo, you've got a blue car! You're playing for Liverpool, not Everton, so get rid of it!"'*

Ron Yeats receives the cold sponge from Bob Paisley during a 1965/66 derby game.

Despite the fact that they weren't among the highest earners in the League, the vast majority of Shankly and Busby's players look back with fond affection on their careers at Liverpool and Manchester United during the period that these two legends of British football were in charge. *'Shankly played for the love of football and so did we. We just thought we might have got a few bob more'*, reflected Ian St John. Shankly did admit to St John in later years that he should have got them better wages. Back at the start of the 1965/66 season, however, there was a considerable amount of dissatisfaction at Anfield, and Cliff Lloyd, the secretary of the Players' Association, was called in to assist the Liverpool team in their wage negotiation. Questioned about the dispute, Lloyd told the press *'I deny as emphatically as possible the rumours being put about that all Liverpool players are seeking a basic wage of £100 per week. Their basic wage, far from being in three figures, has not ever been half that sum.'* Bill Shankly said: *'It would be a pity if differences of this sort were to create unease where no uneasiness has existed in the past.'* Sources close to the players claimed that the Liverpool team were seeking a larger basic wage. If that wasn't forthcoming, they wanted a bonus payment that they considered their performances during the past season deserved. Liverpool's wage dispute dragged on for a few more weeks until the club's Annual Shareholders' Meeting on 14 August. It was there that an announcement was made that all of the squad had now signed new contracts for the coming season. Shankly told the shareholders: *'I would like to pay tribute to the chairman, the president and the board for giving the players one of the finest deals I have ever known in the game.'* If Ian St John was only on a £40 per week basic wage six years later in 1971, the deal that had been struck then was obviously still based on bonus incentives.

Shankly went on to talk about his optimism for the coming season, predicting: *'I can't see why we shouldn't win something next year but I won't try to say what it will be. A lot of tension will leave the team because they have already established themselves as individuals and as a team. Until you get honours, you are always struggling. Now that we have achieved them, we should do even better. Players such as Yeats, Hunt and Byrne are now reaching maturity. They should be at their peak. I reckon a player is best when he is around the twenty-seven mark.'*

As Shankly predicted, Hunt, Yeats and Byrne were once again crucial players in another successful season at Anfield. Roger Hunt in particular was in stunning form, and by the time the first Merseyside derby of the season was due in late September, Hunt had already knocked in eight goals. Prior to the Everton game, Shankly, who lived within yards of Everton's training ground at Bellefield, had been dropping hints that he had been spying on them training from his bedroom window. *'They look absolutely knackered. Harry Catterick had got them running lap after lap around their training ground'*, he would say to Bob Paisley, his players only a few yards away, taking in every word. *'Get to the bookies, Bob. Put a few pounds on us, we're going to murder them!'* When Harry Catterick's team arrived at Anfield on the afternoon of the game, Shankly stood in his usual spot at the players' entrance greeting the opposition as they filed past him. Sometimes, he would get one of the Anfield staff to knock on the dressing-room door of the away team and hand them a box of toilet rolls with the words *'Mr Shankly said you'll be needing these.'* It was tongue-in-cheek, but as the Liverpool players of the period will confirm, it often did send them out on to the field with a psychological advantage over the opposition.

The famous THIS IS ANFIELD sign over the entrance to the pitch was another Shankly ploy to gain an advantage over the opposition before the game had even begun. It told the opposition: once you step past this sign, there is no turning back. Shankly sent his team out to face Everton in the 1965 derby feeling that they were about to take on a bunch of leaden-footed geriatrics. His ploy worked a treat as they thrashed Everton 5-0, the in-form Hunt scoring two.

Shankly would use his brilliant mind and oratorical skills to try to gain an advantage away from the football field as well. At FA disciplinary hearings, he would always try and accompany whichever Liverpool player was appearing: *'He would speak so eloquently and convincingly that members of the commission must have felt that the wrong man had been brought before them!'* recalled Ted Croker, who was secretary of the FA during Shankly's period at Liverpool.

The razor-sharp wit of Shankly was never more evident than on one occasion in the late 1960s when one of England's World Cup heroes, Alan Ball, was the idol of the blue half of Merseyside. Alan's father was manager of Preston at the time and contacted Shankly to see if he wanted to accompany him to a midweek game at Wrexham. The Liverpool boss, always keen to take any opportunity to watch football, agreed to go but said he would follow Alan Ball Snr in his own car to enable him to drive home before the game finished. Shankly was uncertain of the directions to Wrexham, so Ball Snr agreed that Shankly could follow him. When he turned up at Shankly's house, the Liverpool boss was pleased to see that Alan Ball Jnr was in the car with his father. Shankly thought the world of Ball as a player and would have loved to have brought him to Anfield. When the two cars reached the Mersey Tunnel, Shankly, following a short distance behind Ball Snr, was struggling to keep up and ground to a halt halfway through the tunnel. Shankly may have been a great football manager, but he was renowned for his lack of driving skills and was rather accident-prone. Ball Snr pulled up and walked back to Shankly, who was struggling to restart his car. Try as he may, Shankly couldn't get the car to go. *'I tell you what, Bill'*, said the concerned Ball Snr, *'I've got a rope in the boot. I'll attach it to your car and tow you to the tunnel exit. We'll then call a mechanic to sort out the problem.'* Shankly paused for a few seconds, thinking over Ball Snr's suggestion and then exclaimed: *'I don't think that's a good idea, son. Can you imagine the bloody headlines in tomorrow night's Echo if the press find out: 'BILL SHANKLY DRAGGED OUT OF THE MERSEY TUNNEL BY THE BALLS!'*

Whether Shankly managed to get to Wrexham that winter night is unknown, but his Liverpool team were having no difficulty sweeping aside all that came before them during the 1965/66 season. The Christmas holiday period found them facing arch-rivals Leeds both at home and away. They lost the first encounter at Anfield, but then travelled to Elland Road the following day and won 1-0. Both were bruising encounters, as Liverpool against Leeds games during this period inevitably were. Tommy Smith said: *'Every time we played Leeds, it was always a battle. Sometimes the football went by the board.'* The *Liverpool Echo* raved about Smith's performance against Leeds during Liverpool's 1-0 victory, proclaiming: *'Smith is a frightening figure as he goes for the ball, with the undoubted intention of obtaining it at any cost. This sturdy young man gives the impression he would cheerfully charge through a brick wall, head first, if he thought it was necessary.'*

Their victory over Leeds found the Liverpool team in good heart as they set off across the Pennines for their journey back to Merseyside. Bill Shankly's thoughtfulness when it came to the welfare of the Liverpool supporters was always in evidence during his period at the club, but an incident occurred after the Leeds game that illustrates just what the fans meant to him. The Liverpool team bus had travelled a few miles when Shankly spotted some young

The famous THIS IS ANFIELD sign erected at Anfield by the players' entrance to the pitch. This was another one of Shankly's psychological ploys that he hoped would undermine the opposition.

Liverpool fans hitch-hiking. *'Pull over'* Shankly ordered the driver when he spotted the teenagers. He opened the coach door and told the surprised fans to climb on board. Space was made for them to sit down. The Liverpool boss then shouted to someone to bring the boys some packs of sandwiches which were always carried for the return journey home: *'There you are, boys, eat them and when you've finished, go and get your idols' autographs.'* The gobsmacked kids must have thought they were in heaven as they looked around them at their heroes they had only ever seen from afar. After dropping the teenagers off in the city centre, Shankly checked that they had enough money to travel their final distance home. Shankly thought no more of it until one of the boys' parents turned up at Anfield the next day to thank him in person for looking after his son. *'It's me, sir, who should be thanking you for allowing your child to support the club. Not you thanking me'*, Shankly told the man. When news of gestures such as this spread, it was no wonder that Shankly was rapidly becoming a living legend to the Anfield faithful.

Liverpool's European Cup-Winner's Cup campaign had started well during the 1965/66 season, particularly when one considers that in the preliminary round they had to take on Italian giants Juventus. The first leg was in Italy and Liverpool did well to hold Juventus to a one-goal defeat. In the return leg, the Anfield attendance of 51,000 gave the Italians a hot reception. The Kop serenaded Juventus with a rendition of *'Go Back to Italy'*, and roars of laughter when the proposed national anthems of both teams failed to materialise saw both teams, who were standing in line, look bemused by the whole event. The atmosphere was electric, with streams of fainting spectators being stretchered out of the ground for medical attention. When similar scenes of fainting spectators were witnessed by Shankly later in the competition against Celtic, it was little wonder that thoughts were formulating in Shankly's mind that perhaps a move away from Anfield to a bigger venue would be the only answer to the problem of overcrowding at the ground. It would be several years, however, before he would talk to the press about this proposal. Goals from full-back Chris Lawler, who throughout his Anfield career had a habit of popping up with crucial goals, and Mr Versatility, Geoff Strong, won the tie for Liverpool. Once again, as after the Inter Milan game, the Italian press went crazy over Liverpool and their fans. *'Liverpool were unbeatable tonight, crushing Juventus like almonds in a nutcracker. A pity the cold Juventus fans weren't here to see just how much hot passionate support Anfield gives their team,'* raved one Italian paper. Another spoke of Liverpool's football superiority: *'Liverpool gave Juventus a football lesson, playing with vigour and verve. They never once resorted to foul tactics or appeared as if they would get the boot in. The crowd never tried to intimidate Juventus, even if they did sing "Go back to Italy" to the well-known "Santa Lucia" tune. The much-feared Anfield crowd showed they are good sports at heart. Juventus were swept aside by Shankly's red devils.'* Further victories against Standard Liège and Honved set Liverpool up for a semi-final clash with Jock Stein's Celtic. The 'Battle of Britain' would prove to be a memorable clash.

In the League, Liverpool were powering their way to another Championship, including a period in February when they scored four goals in successive games against Blackburn, Sunderland and Blackpool, Roger Hunt netting six of them. With the Championship practically ready to enter the Liverpool trophy cabinet yet again, Shankly turned his attention to Celtic and his old pal Jock

The Kop overflows at Anfield during the Liverpool *v.* Celtic European Cup Winners' Cup second leg game 1966. Liverpool won the tie 2-1 on aggregate.

Stein. *'Celtic were a bloody good side'*, recalls Ron Yeats, *'but Shanks had done his homework and we sat back instead of our usual cavalier approach.'* Celtic put Liverpool under intense pressure, but a Bobby Lennox goal was all they had to show for their bombardment of the Liverpool goal. Though unhappy to lose any game, a smiling Shankly told the press that the pitch didn't really suit Liverpool's style. *'I'm quite certain that Jock had got the ground staff to polish it before the game, to help Celtic's chances'*, was Shankly's bizarre, but very much tongue-in-cheek, accusation.

Five days later at Anfield, Liverpool attempted to overcome Celtic's one-goal lead in front of a 54,000-plus attendance, their highest home gate of the season, and Anfield was full to capacity several hours before kick-off. The Celtic contingent took over the Anfield Road end, many bringing in bottles of liquor. As the game progressed on a damp Merseyside evening, there was the spectacle again of casualties from the Kop having to clamber onto the touchline area to escape the crush. One man suffered a heart attack and an estimated 200 supporters had to receive treatment for minor injuries and fainting. A large proportion of these injuries were sustained when a Celtic goal that would have levelled the tie was disallowed for offside. Bottles rained down on to the pitch at the

Anfield Road end, many of the missiles injuring Celtic fans at the front of the terrace. Earlier, goals from Smith and Strong won the tie for Liverpool but Liverpool found themselves in front of the European Football Association for the bottle-throwing incident, and they were issued with the following statement: *'We will warn Liverpool that stern measures will be taken if there is any repetition. The home club are responsible for the conduct of spectators. We also deprecate spectators invading the field with the games being shown on television. Any club responsible for such indiscretions will be firmly dealt with.'* Liverpool, understandably, were furious that their name was tarnished in this way. Chairman Sidney Reakes commented: *'It's diabolical. It was the hooligans from Scotland who caused the trouble. The Liverpool fans were first class.'* During the clean-up of the bottles littering the ground the following morning, it was estimated that over 4,000 bottles had been thrown. At one stage during the incident, the Kop actually began to chant 'Behave yourselves' to the Celtic fans at the other end of the ground.

Events at Anfield off the field of play ensured that the 'Battle of Britain' would be remembered for many years to come (for all the wrong reasons), but at least Liverpool were now in sight of the first European trophy in their history. Their opponents in the final of the European Cup Winners' Cup were to be Borussia Dortmund and the game would take place at Hampden Park.

Shortly after the Celtic game, Liverpool clinched their second League Championship under Shankly with a 2-1 victory over Chelsea. The Kop were ecstatic, and Chelsea boss Tommy Docherty agreed wholeheartedly with Shankly when the Liverpool manager declared after the game that the Anfield faithful were the best supporters in the world, despite the fact that the Kop taunted Docherty's team mercilessly throughout the ninety minutes with chants of 'Show them the Way to Go Home' and 'London Bridge is Falling Down, Poor Old Chelsea'. Horace Yates of the *Liverpool Echo* saluted Docherty's team before he too commented on the uniqueness of the Anfield fans: *'Football abounds in this Chelsea outfit and Liverpool could not have wished for more sporting rivals to share these*

Phil Chisnall in action for Liverpool in the European Cup Winners' Cup game against Celtic, 1966. Celtic won the first leg 1-0.

magical moments. They lined up to clap Liverpool onto the field (yes, Ron 'Chopper' Harris was playing!) *and it was handshakes all round before they left it.'* Turning his attention to the Anfield fans, Yates said: *'Bill is right! There's no football crowd anywhere to compare with the vast Anfield throng for their fervour, their ability to make the most of the occasion, any occasion, great or small, their spontaneous humour and abundant wit. Entirely original, they are not so much part of a scene, as scene-stealers.'* After applauding the Liverpool players as they paraded around a jubilant Anfield, a chant grew louder and louder until the object of their adulation appeared on the pitch – 'Shankly, Shankly, Shankly' was the cry. Out stepped the Liverpool manager on to the Anfield turf to wave to his adoring army of Anfield fans. They understood entirely the major part that the fanatical Scot had played in the euphoria they were now experiencing. *'To hear the crowd chanting his name, and cheering him puts him in a class apart among managers. I doubt very much if any boss, anywhere in the world, had ever been held in greater esteem – and in saying that, I do not forget the reverence that is felt for Matt Busby at Old Trafford'*, said Yates.

Asked about his relationship with the Anfield fans, Shankly replied: *'I'm just one of the people who stands on the Kop. They think the same as I do, and I think the same as they do. It's a kind of marriage of people who like each other.'* Chairman Sidney Reakes was overjoyed at yet another success, and aware that perhaps he was witnessing the pinnacle of the present team's achievements he commented: *'Liverpool are the finest team in Britain and among the greatest club sides I have seen. For years to come dads will be telling their sons, "You should have seen Liverpool in the 1960s. They were the kings of football".'*

It's incredible to note that during Liverpool's successful League campaign of 1965/66, they used only fourteen players, a testimony to Shankly's claims that not only were they the fittest team in the League, but also that they very rarely suffered from injuries. With the Championship in the bag, Liverpool now turned their attention to winning their first European trophy. Over 25,000 of their supporters set off for Glasgow in the hope of being present when their team completed an historic double. The match was actually only attended by a 41,000 crowd, with any neutral support that was available from the Scottish contingent going to the German side. *'I could never believe that the neutrals supported the Germans. I'll never forgive them for*

Ron Yeats with the First Division Championship trophy 1966. Yeats once said of Bill Shankly: *'Bill took Liverpool by the throat and made it great. It is all very well for managers to take over clubs when they are doing well, when all the structures for success are already there. When Bill came to Anfield it was falling apart – the team and the stands. He was a great man in football and he was a lovely man outside football too.'*

Above: Roger Hunt watches as a goalbound shot is pushed over the bar in the European Cup Winners' Cup final against Borussia Dortmund, 1966. The Germans won the trophy 2-1.

Below: Held scores for Dortmund in the 1966 European Cup Winners' Cup final against Liverpool.

that!' commented Ron Yeats, still bitter many years after the final. Torrential rain virtually turned the Hampden pitch into a quagmire and this resulted in the game developing into a battle of attrition. Atrocious conditions severely restricted Liverpool's passing style and despite continuous pressure, the disciplined German side took the trophy 2-1 after extra time. Shankly was bitterly disappointed and refused to give Borussia any credit at all after the game. *'That lot would be hard pushed to hold a place in the English First Division. We were beaten by a team of frightened men. The two goals they scored were flukes'*, were just some of Shankly's post-match comments. *'It was obviously their plan from the start simply to keep us in subjection'*, Shankly went on, *'they had no real attacking plan, but they won, and I am quite sincere when I say that they are the worst team we met in the competition this season.'*

Despite Shankly's tirade against Borussia, some of his players now acknowledge that when it came to European competition, at least, Shankly was still, at times, tactically naive. Ian St John recently recalled: *'The cavalier attitude that Shanks had wasn't, at the end of the day, going to work for us. We thought there must be a more subtle way. Shanks found it hard to think defensively; he thought teams were going to have an advantage over us if we thought defensively. Shanks' attitude was that we were going to murder everyone. We missed out in the European Cup semi-final and European Cup Winners' Cup final, though I think the players let the management down on that one.'*

The Liverpool supporters' reputation for sportsmanship and good behaviour also took a knock after the Borussia defeat. A section of the Liverpool fans booed the German side and several bottles were thrown as they ran their lap of honour. There were also twenty arrests for breach of the peace. Prior to the game, mystery raiders had scaled the Hampden walls in the early hours of the morning and painted the goalposts red. The words 'Liverpool Champions' and 'Roger Hunt' were also scrawled in red on the boundary walls by the midnight raiders.

10

THE BARREN YEARS

With the exception of Hunt, Callaghan and Byrne, who were on World Cup duty with the England squad, Shankly and the rest of the Liverpool players sat back to enjoy the summer break and the imminent World Cup tournament. Scottish stars Ian St John and Willie Stevenson were invited to make a cameo appearance in the popular BBC sitcom *Till Death Us Do Part*. Merseyside was on a football high with Everton completing a Scouse monopoly of English football's domestic honours by taking the FA Cup after a thrilling final against Sheffield Wednesday. Shankly once declared that Merseyside football fans deserved only the best; 1966 was the year when they got just that. Everton boss Harry Catterick was a great manager in his own right, with two Championships and an FA Cup victory to his credit. Catterick would often get irritable about Shankly's ability to use the press and media to his own and Liverpool's advantage, and once angrily exclaimed *'It's not my fault if I haven't got a voice like Rob Roy!'* in answer to a probing question about his Scottish adversary across Stanley Park at Anfield. Quite soon after his retirement from football, Shankly invariably received a standing ovation from Evertonians if he was spotted at Goodison Park. This was a unique phenomenon indeed, comparable to Alex Ferguson receiving an ovation at Manchester City. Shankly once proclaimed that he'd be proud to be called a Scouser. It wasn't said

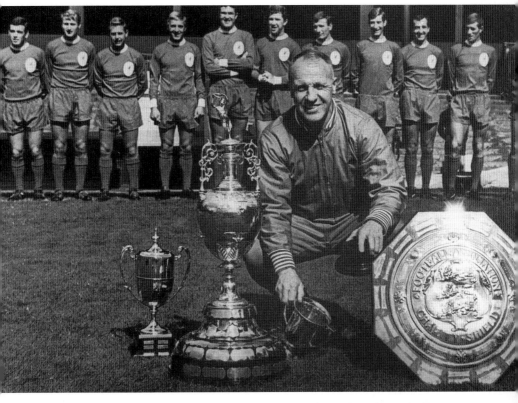

Bill Shankly with his First Division title-winning team of 1966. From left to right: St John, Callaghan, Hunt, Milne, Thompson, Yeats, Lawler, Smith, Strong, Byrne, Stevenson, Lawrence.

for effect – he meant it. Whether red or blue, the people of Merseyside knew Shankly's tribute applied to all of them and they never forgot this.

With Liverpool's Championship victory and Everton's FA Cup triumph, the success for England in the World Cup meant that for Merseyside football fans, that year will probably be at the zenith of their football memories. One man not impressed with the World Cup, however, was Shankly himself; he had always maintained that there was nothing to fear from the rest of the world and was pleased that England had taken the trophy, but he found the standard of play during the tournament sterile and lacking in passion: '*It proved to me that if English clubs wanted to play the continentals at their own defensive game, we would beat them, Liverpool included. But would English fans pay to watch that kind of football every week? In general, I thought the World Cup was played in a negative sense and England won with negative football!'* To Shankly, who had just presided over a Liverpool team winning the title by playing entertaining attacking football for the full ninety minutes, the way one achieved success was as important as the victory itself. He once said: *'There's only two ways to play football, the right way and the wrong way.'* World Champions or not, the only way that Shankly wanted his teams to play was in an entertaining and attacking way, and his two great friends Sir Matt Busby and Jock Stein were of a like mind.

In today's football, where the right result takes precedence above anything else in the game because of the vast amount of finance at stake, Shankly, Busby and Stein would have understood why there was the media euphoria after England's dull 0-0 draw against a substandard Italian team in Rome, but they would have been saddened and left cold by what now constitutes a great performance. Whether Shankly enjoyed the World Cup or not, English football was on a high when the 1966/67 season began, and he reiterated that there was nothing to be learnt from the World Cup. He told the local press: *'We have watched these World Cup teams play and watched them training. But don't think we are going to copy any of their methods. We will prepare and train in the way we've always done, in a manner best suited to our players.'* Ron Yeats said he was certain Liverpool would win another trophy: *'I don't know what, but I hope it will be the European Cup.'* But unbelievably, Shankly's first great team had peaked, and Liverpool were destined to wait another six seasons before they would win another major honour.

The annual curtain-raiser to the new season, the Charity Shield, saw Liverpool at Goodison Park to take on neighbours Everton. Roger Hunt and Ray Wilson, both members of England's successful World Cup team, paraded the trophy in front of 63,000 triumphant Merseysiders. Liverpool won the trophy with a goal from Roger Hunt, and a successful season was anticipated by all at Anfield. They

Kop hero, Roger Hunt, signs for fans after another great victory, 1966.

started well enough with a victory over Leicester, but defeats at Manchester City and an Alan Ball-rejuvenated Everton set them back. There were also problems for them off the field of play after the club decided to ban television cameras from the ground. Liverpool had decided to enforce the ban after fears that television coverage would lead to falling attendance. Everton had also imposed a television blackout at Goodison Park. Liverpool fans were furious at the club's decision. Many of them had difficulties getting into Anfield on big match days, the gates usually being shut well before kick-off time. Petitions against the television ban were organised throughout the city, one in particular from close on 10,000 workers at the Ford car factory stating that unless the ban was lifted, then supporters would be encouraged to boycott all Liverpool matches. One irate fan proclaimed: *'This is ridiculous. It's something I didn't expect from Liverpool. We have yet to hear a plausible reason from the club for their attitude – the old excuse about dwindling crowds just won't do. The opposite is the case at Anfield. It will be difficult for me and the other Liverpool supporters at the plant to stay away but it will show how strongly we feel about it.'* Liverpool's growing band of supporters from outside

Action from the Liverpool v. Ajax away leg in the European Cup, 1966.
Shankly's team were thrashed 7-3 over the two legs by the Johan Cruyff-inspired
Dutch masters.

the Merseyside area were particularly enraged by not being able to
see their heroes on television and sent letters of protest to the
Liverpool Echo. One stated: *'I hope that for the sake of exiled supporters
like myself, the club will reconsider this decision. So far as I can judge, outside
the Merseyside area, Liverpool aren't considered a great team. They aren't,
as I think they should be, compared with Busby's team of the late 1940s
and mid-1950s. Nor the Spurs double-winning team, or even Wolves,
England's first conquerors of top-class European competition. To gain this
deserved reputation, Liverpool need the medium of TV, for after all, there is
as much satisfaction to be gained from national recognition as that given by
local fans.'* This staunch display of 'people power' caused the
Liverpool board to rethink their decision, and the ban on television
cameras was lifted. With a televised thrashing at the hands of Ajax
only weeks away, however, perhaps the powers that be at Anfield
wished they had enforced the ban a short while longer!

Shankly had every reason to feel confident that Liverpool would have a major part to play in that season's European Cup. He had always maintained that a player is at his best when he is twenty-seven or twenty-eight-years old. With many of his squad fitting into this category, Shankly's first great team should have been at their peak, but Liverpool started their campaign nervously. They had to get past Romanian Champions Petrolul Ploesti in the preliminary round. They won the first leg at Anfield 2-0, but lost 3-1 in the return. A third game was needed and Liverpool, through goals from St John and Thompson, won a place in the next round. They were drawn to meet Dutch Champions Ajax next and not too many problems were anticipated. Dutch football wasn't regarded as particularly strong, and Liverpool fans had more fun joking about the name of the Dutch Champions, which was the same as a well-known brand of toilet cleaner. After Liverpool's humiliation at the hands of the Dutch team, Evertonians had fun at the expense of Liverpool for years to come with jibes like, 'How do you flush Liverpool down the toilet? Sprinkle them with Ajax!'

One of Liverpool's concerns before the game was the part, if any, that a nihilistic group who were causing the Dutch authorities a lot of concern would play. During a recent international match between Holland and Czechoslovakia, the 'Provos', as the nihilists called themselves, had invaded the playing area and fought with the police and other fans. As a result, the pitch at the Olympic Stadium, where the Liverpool game would take place, was barricaded with coils of barbed wire. As it turned out, the only pitch invader that dank, foggy night was Shankly himself. Another precaution taken by the Dutch authorities was a 100ft tunnel of unbreakable glass to prevent the players being hit by bottles when the players walked out on to the pitch. Although the Ajax club claimed it wasn't their supporters who were to blame for the recent trouble at the ground, the authorities were taking no chances and an ultimatum was issued to them that if there was any more trouble, football would no longer be allowed at the Olympic Stadium. On the night of the game, a fog descended on Amsterdam and Shankly argued with match officials

The dynamic Peter Thompson in action for Liverpool in the late 1960s. *'The first year I was there we were Champions, the second year the FA Cup, the third Champions again, and the fourth year we finished fifth. That's when Shanks called a crisis meeting! It was a lovely place to be'*, said Thompson.

that the game should be called off. Shankly's pleas were to no avail and the game went ahead. Visibility was, in fact, so poor that Shankly at one stage wandered on to the pitch to issue instructions to his players. *'You couldn't see the game at all'*, he said. *'I was on the pitch. We were 2-0 down, so I went out on to the pitch to have a word with my players and the referee never even saw me.'* Liverpool ended up being beaten 5-1, and although the conditions made the game farcical, there was no doubting that Ajax contained some outstanding talent; notably nineteen-year-old future soccer legend Johann Cruyff. As expected, Shankly was furious after the game. *'We never play well against defensive teams!'* he told the incredulous press.

Remarkably, Shankly convinced the Liverpool supporters that the four-goal deficit could be overcome and close on 54,000 packed into Anfield in the hope of witnessing one of the greatest comebacks of all time. Despite the fact that Shankly had branded them a defensive team, Ajax manager Rinus Michels told the press that he wasn't impressed with the Liverpool defence and expected to score more goals. Dutch wonderboy Cruyff was ill for several games before the return leg, but was passed fit to play. Roared on by the Kop, Liverpool swept forward from the start, but were unable to take an early lead. There was the surreal sight of smoke rising from the Kop, and, once again, the all too familiar spectacle of crushed spectators spilling down onto the side of the pitch. A panic ensued and there were even reports of smoke bombs being set off. Thirty were taken to hospital and over 100 were treated by ambulance services at the ground. A police spokesman told the *Liverpool Echo*: *'You could feel the terrific excitement and tension at the beginning of the match and the pressure from the top of the Kop was probably greater than it usually is.'* The crush happened twenty minutes into the match and

From the edge of the penalty area Roger Hunt scores a fantastic goal against Sunderland at Anfield, 1967.

by half-time, the anticipated Liverpool breakthrough had failed to materialise. Two goals from Cruyff, Liverpool responding with a Hunt double, led to Ajax winning the tie 7-3 on aggregate. Roger Hunt was later to claim: *'Little was known about Ajax in those days, but they were a far better side than we imagined.'* Tommy Smith, as usual, was more forthright: *'Ajax were a great side!'* Shankly was still reluctant to praise the rapidly emerging Dutch master of European football. *'They were lucky'*, he exclaimed.

In the Football League, the expected retention of the Championship was also not going Liverpool's way, with a George Best-inspired Manchester United sweeping all before them as they went on to take their second title in two seasons. The FA Cup was also out of Liverpool's reach, an Alan Ball goal putting Everton into the next round at the expense of their city rivals. Shankly had always fiercely rejected any criticism of his team, but new blood was obviously needed to rejuvenate his squad. He had been tracking Blackpool youngster Emlyn Hughes for several months, after witnessing Hughes's debut for the Lancashire club, and was determined to sign him. He had even taken to phoning Hughes on a Sunday morning to tell the youngster that he'd be a Liverpool player soon: *'I'd be just about to make short work of a plate of eggs, bacon and black pudding when the phone would ring. It would be Shanks. "Hey, Emlyn son, don't eat that stuff you've got on your plate there. I'll be signing you shortly. I want you lean and hungry, son. Lean and hungry!" Today, thirty years later, I still associate the smell of bacon frying with the telephone ringing at 8.30 sharp on a Sunday morning'*, said Hughes. Emlyn Hughes would prove to be one of Shankly's key signings as the successful Liverpool team of the 1960s began to disband. He also attempted to sign another emerging youngster, Howard Kendall, from Preston. But Preston had already sold Gordon Milne, Peter Thompson and David Wilson to Liverpool and the Deepdale fans had taken to chanting 'Stay away Shankly' when he was spotted at the ground. Kendall ended up being sold to Everton and Shankly was furious that he hadn't been given the opportunity to put in his bid for the player. During the summer months of 1967, Shankly decided to splash out again and paid £96,000, a considerable sum at the time, for Chelsea's formidable centre forward Tony Hateley. Chairman Sidney Reakes was as hungry as Shankly to win more trophies and was ready to come up with whatever money was needed to achieve success. He said: '*At Anfield, we don't live on memories. What has been done is history and now we are as eager as ever to begin the writing of new pages. We are poised and ready to move just as soon as the market throws up the type of reinforcement we need.*' Shankly reiterated his chairman's desire for further success: '*The Liverpool public have been weaned on success. Anything less would be an insult to them.*' Liverpool were actually well placed to regain the League title until the beginning of March. But only two victories in the final eleven games allowed Manchester United to pull away. The meagre eight goals scored in that eleven-game sequence was enough to tell Shankly that more firepower was needed up front. Everybody at Anfield, at the beginning of the 1967/68 season, anticipated that Tony Hateley would provide the much needed goals to enable Liverpool to take the title again. He started his Anfield career well enough, with a hat-trick in his third game, a 6-0 drubbing of Newcastle. It would be the darling of the Kop, Roger Hunt, however, who would still provide the bulk of Liverpool's goals. To accommodate Hateley, Liverpool changed their style of play from their quick passing game to a more direct method, belting the ball out quickly to the wing for Callaghan or Thompson to whip over crosses. It was hoped that the formidable heading ability of Hateley would net him a bagful of goals, but the plan never really succeeded.

In the Inter Cities Fairs Cup, Liverpool began their campaign well enough, with victories over Malmo and TSV Munchen. In the next round, they were drawn against Hungarian team Ferencvaros, who had just won their domestic League Championship with twenty-four victories in twenty-seven games. Ferencvaros also included nine of the current Hungarian team in their line-up. The first leg was due to be played in Hungary. With the onset of the harsh Hungarian winter only days away, Liverpool agreed to a 1 p.m. kick-off to enable them to fly back to Liverpool directly after

Roger Hunt races through on goal at a snow-swept Anfield in 1968. Liverpool's opponents were Ferencvaros in a Fairs Cup third round tie.

the game. They did well to hold the talented Hungarians to a 1-0 defeat, but first there was another hazardous journey back to Liverpool to contend with. The general consensus is that throughout the Shankly era, the Liverpool boss disliked the Ionian treks abroad and hated flying in particular. The flight home from Budapest was another nail-biting affair. The Liverpool squad had to stay sealed in their plane while ground crew cleared snow, ice and slush from the runway. The wings of the aircraft then had to be de-iced in a snow blizzard before an attempted take off was possible. Thankfully, the plane was able to depart during its first attempt. While in mid-air, Shankly, now in a more relaxed frame of mind, was informed that it had been touch and go as to whether the airport was going to have to be closed due to the hazardous conditions. At times like this, it was no wonder that the Liverpool manager would ask himself if football really was more important than life and death. In the return leg at Anfield, Ferencvaros took an early lead and held out to take the tie 2-0 on aggregate. Europe had once again proved to be Shankly's Achilles heel. Leeds United, by now an outstanding team, actually went on to beat Ferencvaros in the final of the Fairs Cup towards the end of the 1967/68 season. Shankly would have to wait several more seasons before his team would triumph in Europe.

Liverpool ended their League programme in third place to Joe Mercer's Manchester City. A rethink was clearly needed if Liverpool were to challenge for the game's top honours again. Although no trophies came Liverpool's way in 1968, their balance sheet for the season was showing a healthy profit. Gate receipts alone brought in £395,000 with Liverpool being the third best-supported team in the country behind Manchester United and Everton. Shankly knew that money would be available to strengthen the team and in September he decided to make Wolves' promising youngster Alun Evans his boldest signing to date. Evans cost £100,000, a record fee for a teenager. Part of this money had been recouped a few weeks earlier by off-loading Tony Hateley to Coventry for £80,000. Apart from rebuilding his team, Shankly had other things on his mind during the summer of 1968. The welfare of Liverpool's supporters was always uppermost in his thoughts, and although since his arrival at Liverpool in 1959 there had been major improvements at the ground, to

Geoff Strong attacks the Ferencvaros goal during the 1968 Fairs Cup game.

Shankly it was still not good enough for the Anfield faithful. The Kop was a unique phenomenon, and created an atmosphere that couldn't be bettered anywhere in the world. But the sight of crushed fans, laid out on the side of the pitch, gasping for breath, had occurred all too often, particularly during big match nights in Europe, for Shankly's taste. The Liverpool boss began to make noises about the unthinkable – Liverpool moving from their beloved Anfield. For a long time, residents who lived near to Anfield, in the narrow streets that surrounded the ground, had been resentful about being virtual prisoners in their own homes on match days. There were even reports in the press of violent clashes between residents and Liverpool fans before and after the game. Much of the aggravation was caused by fans queuing to get in. One resident of Kemlyn Road told the local press: *'There's no good will at all for Liverpool FC in the roads round the ground. For too long the club has walked with hobnailed boots over the residents. This can't go on any longer and we are asking the chief constable to protect the district.'* Another resident stated: *'I'm a great fan of Liverpool and love to see them win, but I don't go to matches any more because of the discomfort and rowdyism. If any other private company treated residents in a similar way, they would have been prosecuted long ago.'* What upset the residents the most was the foul language and their passageways being used as public conveniences. From the club and Shankly's point of view, there was also the fact that on many occasions, particularly for big matches, the gates were locked at Anfield well before kick-off time. The ground simply wasn't big enough for the growing number of supporters who wanted to watch Liverpool, and this meant that potential revenue was lost to the club. With all of these factors in mind, it was no wonder that Shankly was thinking hard about the possibility of leaving Anfield. *'I would far rather stay at Anfield of course'*, he told the *Daily Post*. *'If only we could provide seats for 40,000 what a ground that would be, with its unmatched atmosphere. But the comfort of our followers is something which concerns me deeply. These people, who are prepared to stand in all weather throughout the season in all manner of climatic trials deserve a reward. They deserve a seat.'* He even told the interviewer where a new stadium could be situated: *'If we could build a 100,000 seater stadium at Aintree, to be shared with Everton, then I would be tempted to move from Anfield.'* After the Hillsborough tragedy, Liverpool, of course, did turn Anfield into an all-seater stadium. But it's interesting to note that way back in 1968, the visionary Shankly, with the safety and comfort of his beloved Liverpool supporters in mind, was prepared to contemplate an exodus from Anfield to share a new stadium with city rivals Everton.

One place that had been drastically improved since Shankly's arrival in 1959 was Liverpool's training headquarters at Melwood. There was now a new pavilion, treatment room, saunas and an all-weather pitch equipped with floodlights. Back in 1959, there hadn't even been running water available. Welcoming his squad back for preseason training, Shankly gave a warm reception to the new group of youth players that had joined the club. *'You have joined a great club with the finest traditions'*, he said. *'Here we have no interest in politics or religion. It doesn't matter what you are so long as you can play football. The Liverpool club success has been based on hard work and simplicity. That is the motto here and it will continue to be so.'* He concluded his pep talk by telling the youngsters not to be afraid to ask the senior players for help and advice. *'Don't hesitate to approach the players'*, he told them. *'They know all the answers. These men have been among the most successful players in Britain for the last six years. They know the game. Talk to them.'* Not all of the youths at Liverpool during the Shankly years, however, were won over by the Scot's fanatical style of management. Paul Fairclough, the manager of non-League Stevenage during their headline-grabbing FA Cup run in the 1997/98 season, was a sixteen-year-old member of Liverpool's C team during the mid-1960s. After one defeat, Shankly was livid and burst into the dressing room to tell the youngsters what he thought of them. Fairclough recalled: *'He strode in, thumped the desk, smashed a cup and came round criticising each one of us close to our faces. When he got to me, I just laughed out loud because I thought he was a madman. He went totally ballistic. I just couldn't take on board this man getting so worked up about football. I'd love to say I got swept along with the Shankly era at Liverpool, but really I can't say I learned anything. It's quite sad but I didn't.'*

Left: Emlyn Hughes, Tommy Smith and Peter Thompson set off on another European adventure in the late 1960s.

Opposite: Liverpool go out of the European Fairs Cup on the toss of a coin against Athletic Bilbao in 1968.

The 1968-69 season began slowly for Liverpool with three victories in their first seven games. The introduction of Alun Evans into the team in September, however, coincided with Liverpool stepping up a gear. They won five games in succession, scoring 18 goals and conceding none in the process. Evans looked destined to become the new idol of Anfield. In Europe, Liverpool were confident they could overcome the Spanish club Athletic Bilbao in the Fairs Cup. The first leg in Spain resulted in a 2-1 defeat. The return at Anfield saw Liverpool win by the same score. Ron Yeats stepped into the centre circle to decide who would go through on the toss of a coin. The toss went against Liverpool and they went out. After going out of the FA Cup to Leicester, there was only the League to aim for. At one stage in the season, they actually pulled 4 points clear of eventual Champions Leeds, but an unimpressive run with only two victories in their last seven games saw Don Revie's team overhaul them on their way to a comfortable title victory.

Liverpool finished without a trophy again. The only crumb of comfort for Shankly was the fact that four players were now at Anfield who would become vital ingredients of his next great team: the recently signed Alec Lindsay, who would be converted from an impressive wing half into an outstanding full-back, goalkeeper Clemence and midfielder Brian Hall were biding their time waiting for their chance to impress. Centre half Larry Lloyd had also been snapped up from Bristol Rovers for £50,000 and would eventually take Ron Yeats' place at the heart of the Liverpool defence.

11

THE FINAL PIECE IN THE JIGSAW

Inevitably Shankly's great team of the 1960s began to disband. Players such as Stevenson, Milne and Byrne had already been replaced, and for Lawrence, Strong, Yeats and St John, their Liverpool careers were drawing to a close. Liverpool began the 1969/70 season in great style, winning their opening four games and not tasting defeat until mid-September, away to Manchester United. After that reverse, their results became inconsistent. Roger Hunt and Ian St John struggled to retain their places in the team and discarding them caused Shankly much heart-searching. St John was dropped for an away game at Newcastle and recalls that Shankly was nowhere to be seen when he was told the news: *'Shankly avoided coming into the dressing room until five minutes before the kick-off. I'd been his first big signing at the start of the revolution and he couldn't bear to sit down and say to me, "I'm leaving you out." When I asked him "Why didn't you tell me earlier?", he said "You weren't in the dressing room when I announced the team." He couldn't bear to tell me face to face.'* Bob Paisley claimed that Shankly found it hard to hurt players who had served him with distinction: *'If Bill had one failing, it was the fact that he didn't like to upset players that had done so well for him. He was a softie at heart.'* Shankly had always cultivated the 'tough guy' image, but those who knew him well said it was all a myth. Soccer luminary Joe Mercer had known Shankly since the 1930s and had no doubts that the Scot

Anfield great Ian St John training at Melwood. Bill Shankly said of St John: *'Ian is a footballer with a tiger in his tank. He is a player who has got one thing necessary for success – a heart the size of himself. Men with pluck, fire and outstanding ability like St John can't really fail.'* St John himself recalls that Shankly's words of advice to him when he signed for the club were: 'Don't overeat, and don't lose your accent.'

wasn't the hard man that many thought he was: *'They say he's tough, he's hard, he's ruthless. Rubbish. He's got a heart of gold, he loves the game, he loves his fans, he loves his players. He's like an old Collie dog, he doesn't like hurting his sheep. He'll drive them certainly, but bite them, never.'*

Roger Hunt also found it hard to come to terms with being dropped from the team, the first time being the previous season when Shankly took him off against Leicester. Hunt recalled: *'Ron Yeats approached me and said he thought the management wanted me off. I said words to the effect that they could get stuffed. Then the referee came to me and said I was being called off. I had no choice then. As I passed the bench, I pulled off my shirt and threw it into the dugout before marching straight inside to have a bath.'* Hunt, always the gentleman and a legend at Anfield for as long as Liverpool exists, probably reacted in a way that surprised Shankly, but the Liverpool boss definitely didn't want players at the club who showed no reaction to losing their place.

Above: Two Merseyside footballing greats, Tommy Smith of Liverpool and Everton's Alan Ball, lead out their teams before a 1969 encounter.

Below: Bill Shankly passes on some last-minute instructions to Tommy Smith.

Liverpool ended the season in fifth position, fifteen points behind Champions Everton.

With the prospect of moving to a new 100,000 all-seater stadium at Aintree now no longer on the horizon, ground improvements continued at Anfield in the close season. New floodlights were installed, and, as with everything at Anfield, to Shankly they were the greatest floodlights in the history of the game: *'Wonderful lights! wonderful lights!'* he jubilantly told the local press. *'This is the first time you could really say this ground has been lit up... The effect on the players will be good under these new lights. It will be like coming out on to the pitch on a bright, sunny day. The players are bound to get some sort of boost.'* Shankly's players were gathered round listening to their manager talking about the extra power of the new floodlights, and the new first-team goalkeeper, Ray Clemence, decided there and then that a new cap was needed with a large peak on it. On another occasion, Shankly told an incredulous press: *'Just look at that grass, boys. It's great here at Anfield, professional grass.'*

On the playing front, at the start of the 1970/71 season, with only four wins out of their first eleven games the new floodlights clearly hadn't given the Liverpool team the type of boost Shankly had anticipated. But the dashing winger Steve Heighway, who had been signed for nothing from local amateur team Skelmersdale, would soon be introduced to the team along with John Toshack. Toshack cost Liverpool a £110,000 fee from Cardiff City, but the tall Welshman, along with Heighway, would prove to be an outstanding acquisition for the team. Although Liverpool were never really in contention in the League, Shankly's blossoming new team put together a good run in the FA Cup. Their opponents in the semi-final were Everton. Goals from Evans and Hall in a tense encounter gave Liverpool a 2-1 victory. They were through to Wembley for the first time since 1965, their opponents Arsenal.

Prior to the final, Shankly signed a player who had been strongly recommended to him by his former teammate at Preston, Andy Beattie, who had spotted Kevin Keegan playing for Scunthorpe and was immediately impressed by this darting, irrepressible youngster,

An all-star gathering at Anfield for Roger Hunt's testimonial game in 1972. Over 56,000 attended the game in honour of the Anfield hero they called 'Sir Roger'.

who played his heart out for the full ninety minutes. Shankly got Keegan for £35,000, a sum later described by the Liverpool boss as 'robbery with violence', and the son of a Yorkshire miner would go on to become one of the all-time Liverpool greats. With Ray Clemence also being snapped up from Scunthorpe, and later Keegan, both of whom would go on to become world-class performers, it can't be emphasized enough just what a key role the lowly Yorkshire club played in the construction of Shankly's second great team. With Liverpool back at Wembley, the demand for tickets was as intense as ever. Shankly did his best to try and supply as many genuine Liverpool supporters as he could, but it was always a losing battle. On the day of the game, Liverpool, who had won the toss to play in their normal red strip, took to the field confident they could stop Arsenal completing the League and Cup double for only the second time in the century. Liverpool took the lead through Heighway, but struggled to dominate the game. Shankly had said beforehand, *'We've got to Wembley with a team of boys that will last for ten years.'* With Keegan now in the squad, though unavailable for the final, Shankly did have a squad who would go on to dominate the game throughout the 1970s. But against Arsenal their time hadn't yet come. Arsenal equalised Heighway's effort and went on to win the game through an outstanding Charlie George effort. *'The long-haired George may look like someone who has strayed in from the nearest discothèque, but this boy is a great player'*, said one paper. If Shankly had snapped up Keegan a few months earlier, the player who would go on to galvanise what was obviously a talented team lacking penetration may have given Liverpool victory against a well-organised Arsenal. Tommy Smith recently recalled that he was so disappointed after the 1971 final that he was violently ill after trudging back to

Bill Shankly and his backroom staff attempt to revitalise the Liverpool team as they prepare for extra time in the 1971 FA Cup final. A great Charlie George goal, however, won the cup for Arsenal.

Above: Liverpool captain Tommy Smith and Arsenal's Frank McLintock toss up before the start of the 1971 FA Cup final.

Left: An injured Chris Lawler is helped to his feet by Arsenal players during the 1971 FA Cup Final.

Bill Shankly prepares to give his famous 'Chairman Mao' speech after Liverpool's defeat in the 1971 FA Cup final against Arsenal.

the dressing room. *'I can still remember Charlie George lying on the ground with that smug look on his face after he had scored that crucial goal'*, Smith lamented.

The following day, Liverpool were welcomed back to the city by over 100,000 disappointed fans. Brian Hall remembers that the Liverpool manager was locked deep in thought as he waved to the fans from an open-topped bus. Shankly turned to the young Liverpool player and demanded: *'Hey son, who's that Chinaman, you know the one with the sayings? What's his name?'* The university-educated Hall thought: *'Are you barmy or what?'* Hall told Shankly: *'Is it Chairman Mao you mean?'* *'That's him son'*, replied an excited Shankly. Hall forgot about Shankly's bizarre question until the team arrived at St George's Hall. As thousands flocked around the Victorian building, Shankly came to the microphone and began to speak: *'Ladies and gentlemen, yesterday at Wembley, we may have lost the Cup, but you the people have won everything. You have won over the*

Above: Bill Shankly greets the Liverpool fans before giving his 'Chairman Mao' speech in 1971.

Left: Kevin Keegan pictured sitting outside Anfield waiting to be signed by Liverpool in 1971. Keegan became one of the great Liverpool stars of the 1970s.

policemen in London. You won over the London public, and it's questionable if Chairman Mao's China could have arranged such a show of strength as you have shown yesterday and today.' The multitudes roared their approval. Shankly had the ability to lift his team if they lost, and now he made the Liverpool supporters feel on top of the world after a disappointing Wembley defeat. Shankly knew that something special was needed and came up with the perfect uplifting speech. Brian Hall shook his head and recalls thinking: *'This man's a genius.'*

When Shankly gathered his squad together for the start of the preseason training, before the 1971/72 season, they were both surprised and amused at the new arrival Kevin Keegan. The fanatically keen newcomer wanted to be first in everything. *'I had to simmer him down'*, recalls Shankly. *'"You don't train like that, son", I told him. He wanted to win every race in training. I had to tell him to take it easy, you're only preparing to train.'* Tommy Smith and the other experienced Liverpool first-teamers nicknamed Keegan 'Andy McDaft' but pretty soon they became as bowled over by Keegan as the training staff at Anfield were. Bob Paisley, remembering Keegan's arrival at Anfield, said: *'He had infectious enthusiasm, boundless stamina and seemed to love every kick of the game. Joe Fagan and I were impressed by the fact that he had a buzz about him every time he got the ball.'*

It was originally planned that Keegan would take over the Ian Callaghan role, operating up and down the right hand side of midfield – Callaghan was struggling after a cartilage operation. But as it turned out, the now fit-again Callaghan reverted to his midfield role and Keegan was an instant success playing up front with Toshack. Liverpool opened the season with four wins in their first five games, and prospects looked good for a title-winning season. With double-winners Arsenal competing in the European Cup, Liverpool were England's representatives in the European Cup Winners' Cup. They had the misfortune, however, to draw Bayern Munich in the second round and lost 3-1 on aggregate to the talented Germans. However, Liverpool remained in contention in the League until the final game of the season. An incredible end-of-season run, with thirteen wins in their last sixteen games, saw them come within a whisker of the title, but it was to be Brian Clough's Derby County who would be crowned as Champions.

Liverpool's attack wasn't yet firing on all cylinders, but their defence was developing into the meanest in the League, conceding just 30 goals. Shankly's great team of the 1960s had been built on the 'Attack, Attack, Attack' principle; his next great team was built on a defence that gave nothing away, and exciting forwards like Keegan and Heighway who could create goals out of nothing. During the early 1970s Shankly told an interviewer the type of team he was hoping to develop at Anfield: *'I want to build a team that's invincible, so that they have to send a team from bloody Mars to beat us.'*

The Liverpool team that won the double of the League Championship and UEFA Cup in season 1972/73 could have been just the type of line-up he had in mind. Shankly brought in the excellent Peter Cormack from Nottingham Forest for a £110,000 fee in the summer of 1972 to supplement the squad. The Anfield faithful looked forward to the new season with relish. Shankly and his backroom staff had also developed a style of play that they hoped would minimise the risk of injury. Shankly recalled: *'The team played in sections of the field, like a relay. We didn't want players running the length of the field, stretching themselves unnecessarily, so our back men played in*

Leeds United's Billy Bremner scores a great goal at Anfield to help his team to a Fairs Cup semi-final victory over Liverpool in 1971.

Left: One of Shankly's most impressive signings of the late 1960s, Larry Lloyd. Lloyd took the place of the great Ron Yeats at the heart of the Liverpool defence in the early 1970s. He played 217 times for the Reds and won 4 England caps.

Right: Ray Clemence, an £18,000 capture from Scunthorpe who went on to become the greatest Liverpool goalkeeper of all time. Clemence appeared for Liverpool 656 times and won 61 England caps. Clemence put much of his success down to Bill Shankly. He once said of Shankly: '*They say everybody remembers where they were when Kennedy was killed. It was the same with the news of Shankly's retirement at Liverpool. Shanks was a charismatic bloke and a fantastic motivator, while always trying to keep the game simple.*'

one area, and then passed on to the midfield men in their area, and so on to the front men. So, whilst there was always room for individuals within our system, the work was shared out.'

Four wins in their first five games gave Liverpool a great start to the season. The *Liverpool Echo* was in no doubt that this was going to be a successful season for the team: '*By now, the whole of the First Division will have got the message. It's quite clear – Liverpool are a team to fear this season.*' A female Koppite collated the songs and chants that were popular during this period and some were reproduced in an article she penned for a local paper. She wrote: '*I can't say I'm fond*

Shankly seen here with Liverpool coach Ronnie Moran.

of the song in which they bawl "We only carry hatchets to bury in their 'eads". But the Kop are always quick to spot something new. To Tommy Smith when he trotted out for the first time in white boots, they sang "Where did you get those boots, where did you get those boots?". "Toshack is the king" was sung to the tune of Men of Harlech, and to Malcolm MacDonald during a recent Newcastle visit "Super Mac is only good when its raining" to the tune of "Michael Row the Boat Ashore".'

The Kop were in good voice as Liverpool powered their way to their first title of the 1970s. They had never been content to just watch, they had to be an active part of the communal Anfield experience. They were certainly a part of the celebrations when Shankly and his team paraded around Anfield with the Championship trophy after a goalless draw against Leicester assured them of the title. In Europe too, Liverpool were only two games away from success in the UEFA Cup, after a hard-fought semi-final victory over Spurs. Liverpool's opponents in the final were Borussia Mönchengladbach. The first leg was due to be played at Anfield on 9 May, but torrential rain meant that only twenty minutes' play was possible. John

Toshack had been dropped for the abandoned game and had exchanged words with Shankly. The Welsh player, thinking that his days at Liverpool had probably come to a close, had driven home to tell his wife that he would be looking for a new club soon. Within minutes of arriving home, Shankly was on the phone telling him to prepare himself for that night's rearranged game; the Liverpool manager had spotted the previous night that the Germans had looked vulnerable to high crosses, and Toshack was just the man to exploit this. Brian Hall was the unlucky player who had to make way for Toshack's return. *'I remember that evening vividly because I thought I'd be wearing the same number as the night before'*, recalls Hall. *'Shanks didn't see it that way of course. He decided a tactical change was needed. At the end of the day, Shanks was right because we won 3-0. I'd*

'My idea was to build Liverpool Football Club into a bastion of invincibility. Napoleon had that idea. That's what I wanted. Liverpool would be untouchable, up and up and up until eventually everyone would have to submit.' – Bill Shankly

European success at last. Bill Shankly holds the UEFA Cup after his team's victory over Borussia Mönchengladbach over two legs.

have argued at the time that we would have won 4-0 if I'd played, but I think I'd be being a bit naive if I said that.' In the return leg Borussia Mönchengladbach put Liverpool under severe pressure, but Liverpool held out to take the UEFA Cup 3-2 on aggregate. Shankly, at long last, had won his first European trophy. Although winning the UEFA Cup gave Shankly great pleasure, it was his third League Championship that pleased him the most: *'That was the greatest triumph of all of them. Winning the Championship early on was a novelty. This one was won with a new team. This was definitely the greatest moment that I had in football.'*

Shankly had built a team that would dominate the game for the rest of the 1970s. An estimated 250,000 ecstatic Merseysiders lined the streets of Liverpool as they triumphantly paraded the two trophies through the city. Shankly, wearing a bright-red shirt, had never looked happier. When the motorcade reached Liverpool's Picton Library, the team alighted from their bus and Shankly spoke to the thousands massed in front of the building: *'This is the greatest day of my career. If there is any doubt that you are the greatest fans in the world, this is the night to prove it. We have won for you and that is all we are interested in, winning for you. The reason we have won is because we believe and you believe and it's faith and interest that have won us something. Thank God we are all here. You don't know how much we love you.'*

Above: Ballet in the air at Anfield – John Toshack challenges Chelsea's David Webb and Gary Locke for the ball in 1972.

Below: Anfield great Kevin Keegan. Keegan said of Bill Shankly: *'What Liverpool are today is down to him. A lot of people have made their contributions over the years, but it was Shanks who started it all. He was not one of the greatest men in football I was ever associated with — he was THE greatest.'*

Bill Shankly celebrates with his Liverpool team after clinching the League
Championship in 1973.

John Toshack displays the First Division trophy during a civic reception in 1973.
Toshack gave the Reds great service in the 1970s, making 236 appearances and
scoring 95 goals. He also won 40 caps for Wales.

The dashing Steve Heighway puts the Dynamo Berlin defence under pressure in a UEFA cup-tie during the 1972/73 season. Heighway scored in a 3-1 victory.

Kevin Keegan celebrates his goal against Borussia Mönchengladbach in the UEFA Cup final, 1973. Liverpool won the first leg 3-0 and held on to win the cup 3-2 on aggregate after the away game in Germany.

Above: Liverpool boxer John Conteh displays his World Championship belt and Tommy Smith the UEFA Cup at Liverpool's homecoming tour, 1973.

Opposite: Kevin Keegan at Liverpool's triumphant homecoming after winning the UEFA Cup and the League Championship, 1973.

With that, Shankly led the fans in a spontaneous rendition of *You'll Never Walk Alone,* the anthem of Anfield.

A Liverpool fan, eighty-four-year-old Henry Murphy, who had been following the team since 1904, was asked for his opinions of Shankly. He replied: *'Quite honestly, I can think of no man I admire more than him. I admire him for the same reason everyone admires him and that's for putting Liverpool where they are today and for being a credit to the game.'* If Shankly had called it a day there and then the jubilant Scot couldn't have ended on a happier note. But there was one more great success to come before the legend of Anfield bowed out.

12

LIKE WALKING TO THE ELECTRIC CHAIR

Shankly's emerging young team began the 1973/74 season confident that they could emulate the achievements of Celtic and Manchester United, and bring the European Cup back to British shores. Their defence of the title didn't start too well, however, as they won only four of their first nine games. In the first round of the European Cup they also made an unconvincing start, beating the part-timers of Luxembourg, Jeunesse d'Esch, just 3-1 over the two legs. They were matched against Red Star Belgrade in the next round. Red Star were a useful team, but if Liverpool had played with anything like the same fervour that had swept them to the Championship the previous season, they would have won the tie. As it turned out, Red Star brought to an end Shankly's last crack at the European Cup before it had had a chance to build up momentum, winning the tie 4-2 on aggregate. Liverpool, and in particular the heir-apparent to the manager's chair, Bob Paisley, would gain from the Red Star defeat and learn how to sit back and then hit teams on the break with devastating results. In European competition, patience was most definitely a virtue. Shankly's style of play was based on tactics and passion, and he once described himself as *'an impatient, patient man'*. To win at the highest level in Europe, the European Cup, a tactician was needed whose patient elements of his nature heavily outweighed the impatient parts. Shankly undoubt-

Liverpool's Ray
Clemence guards his
goal at Anfield.

edly laid the foundations for Liverpool's incredible success in
Europe over the next decade; a Geordie with a deep understanding
of the game, Bob Paisley, would build on the foundations that
Shankly had laid.

With the dream of success in the European Cup gone, Liverpool
turned their attention back to domestic competition. They regained
their consistency and pushed Leeds all the way for the
Championship, but the outstanding Yorkshire team couldn't be
overtaken and took the title by 5 points. It was in the FA Cup that
Shankly's team, after some early-round scares, really excelled. They
put out Doncaster, but only after a hard-fought replay in the third
round, and were then drawn against Carlisle. The first game at
Anfield resulted in a 0-0 draw. Liverpool travelled to Brunton Park
expecting a difficult time, but their class came to their aid and they
won comfortably 2-0. After the game, the Carlisle manager Alan

Chris Lawler in action for Liverpool against Red Star Belgrade in the European Cup, 1973. Red Star won the tie 4-2 on aggregate and put an end to Shankly's dream of emulating Jack Stein and Matt Busby in winning the European Cup.

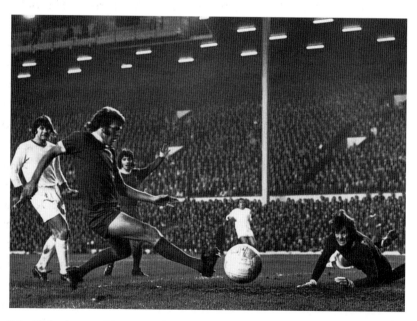

John Toshack goes close to scoring against Red Star Belgrade at Anfield, 1973.

Liverpool defenders Emlyn Hughes and Phil Thompson close down Mick Lyons of Everton at Anfield during the 1973/74 season.

Ashman was asked his opinions on Shankly's Liverpool. He told the press: *'Liverpool are wholehearted. They fit into the Shankly style of play, which is all action. Liverpool and Leeds have been the top two teams over the past ten years. The yardstick of a good side is how they have been playing for years. It amazes me how Liverpool keep it going. I can't see them ever being anything less than a good side. I hope they go on and win the FA Cup.'* In the next rounds, Liverpool defeated Ipswich, Bristol City and Leicester to get to Wembley where their opponents would be Newcastle United, who were as desperate, if not more so, for success. Newcastle hadn't won a domestic trophy since the early 1950s, when they won the FA Cup three years out of five. A classic final was anticipated, particularly when Newcastle's Malcolm MacDonald made it known that he would make sure that the Liverpool defence had a difficult afternoon. He was undoubtedly a formidable player and had once scored a hat-trick against Liverpool. Tommy Smith had sidled up to MacDonald after that game and told him in no uncertain terms that he'd scored his last goal against

Left: Kevin Keegan celebrates another goal for Liverpool during the 1973–74 season.

Right: Steve Heighway heads at goal against Newcastle in the 1974 FA Cup final.

Liverpool. Smith reminded MacDonald of this as the two teams lined up in the Wembley tunnel before the game, and whether this played on MacDonald's mind is unknown, but 'Supermac', as he was known to the Newcastle fans who idolised him, was virtually anonymous throughout the final. Smith, in fact, left MacDonald to Phil Thompson, who had an outstanding game and kept such a firm grip on MacDonald that Tommy Smith spent much of the game foraging up the right wing setting up goalscoring opportunities. Liverpool's emphatic 3-0 victory demonstrated everything that Shankly held dear. Their passing was crisp and precise and up front they had flair and a cutting edge. Goals from Steve Heighway and two from Kevin Keegan gave Liverpool a comfortable victory in one of the most one-sided finals seen at Wembley. After the game, Prime Minister Harold Wilson, who was a genuine football fan and rarely missed a Wembley final, remarked: *'I said before the game that once Keegan and Heighway start moving then the result won't be in doubt.*

I forecast 2-1 to Liverpool before the match. If it had gone on for another ten minutes it might have been 5-0.' The only crumb of comfort for two of the outclassed Newcastle team, McDermott and Kennedy, was that they would soon be joining Liverpool and becoming a part of the successful Anfield scene themselves.

Shankly declined the opportunity to go on his team's lap of honour, and instead stood quietly taking in the euphoria. Several Liverpool fans ignored the team and went up to Shankly and kissed his feet, a spontaneous act of homage to their messiah. There can be little doubt that the Anfield faithful held their team in the highest esteem. But their ultimate acclamation was for a sixty-year-old Scot, a man they worshipped. Interviewed after the game, as he sat quietly tucking into a celebratory pork pie and mug of tea, Shankly said: *'I'm happy, not for me, no. I'm happy for the players, training staff, directors, but above all I'm happy for the multitudes. I'm happy for them because I work for them. I'm just sorry that I couldn't go in among them and speak to all of them. The people who came on to the field and bowed down to me. These are the people I'm pleased for more than anybody else.'* Turning to his team, Shankly knew that he had a squad who could win trophies for several more years: *'The great team of the 1960s won the League in 1964, the Cup in 1965 and the League again in 1966. Without doubt, this is the best team in the League, they can go on to do the same as the 1960s team.'*

Liverpool arrived back on Merseyside to the greatest home-coming they had ever received. An estimated 500,000 lined the streets to welcome home Shankly's Wembley heroes. The Liverpool *Daily Post* agreed with Shankly's sentiments that this team had the potential to become the greatest in the club's history, saying: *'not even this 3-0 hammering paid adequate tribute to the overwhelming might, majesty and ascendancy of Liverpool in a football fantasy that made a Newcastle nightmare in broad daylight. It was a victory which must have ended all those comparisons with the great side of the 1960s. This side can become the greatest of them all. In fourteen years with Bill Shankly, Liverpool have learned to walk with pride. They have never known a finer hour than this.'* Once again, Shankly spoke to the mass of supporters, who listened intently to his every word: *'I think today, I feel prouder*

Kevin Keegan eludes Newcastle's Terry McDermott in the 1974 FA Cup final.

Ian Callaghan and Kevin Keegan parade the FA Cup around Wembley after Liverpool's win over Newcastle, 1974.

From left to right: Steve Heighway, Emlyn Hughes, Bob Paisley, Joe Fagan, Kevin Keegan and Ray Clemence seen here during Liverpool's homecoming tour of the city with the FA Cup.

than I have ever done before. I said three years ago we would go back to Wembley. Not only did the team win the Cup yesterday, they gave an exhibition of football. But above all, we are pleased for you. It's you we play for. It's you who pay our wages. Not only did we win the Cup on the field, but we won it on the terraces as well.'

His final speech to the multitudes was once again greeted with rapturous applause. As the youngest member of the Liverpool team looked around him at the massive crowds that packed the city centre, he found it hard to believe that he was now an established member of the team he had supported from the terraces as a boy. Phil Thompson recalled: *'I remember it in 1965, we were all standing on top of a car watching the team return with the FA Cup. I'm one of the Kop really. I don't know what I'm doing playing for the team. I want to be with the Kop half the time.'* Shankly knew exactly what the Liverpool youngster was doing in the team, but the sentiments expressed by Thompson could have come from the Liverpool boss himself.

Bill Shankly, Steve Heighway, Emlyn Hughes and John Toshack with the FA Cup.

With the FA Cup in the Anfield trophy cabinet, and an outstanding young team who looked destined for further success, Liverpool supporters looked set to enjoy the summer break safe in the knowledge that all was well at Anfield. A surprise press conference was hastily convened at the club on 12 July 1974. News of Shankly's retirement came like a bolt from the blue. When the news hit the airwaves that Bill Shankly had decided to retire, it was met with widespread disbelief. An Evertonian wind-up was the general consensus of those who hadn't yet had it confirmed on their radio sets or television screens. '*Why?*' was the question on everyone's lips, '*He's not ill is he?*' The other announcement that day by the Liverpool board, that they had just purchased Ray Kennedy from Arsenal for £200,000, didn't really concern them, though as it turned out, Kennedy would go on to become one of the greatest midfielders who ever put on a Liverpool shirt. When the news sank in that

Above: Two Liverpool legends, Bob Paisley and Bill Shankly with the FA Cup.

Right: The people of Liverpool display their devotion to Bill Shankly at a street party after the 1974 FA Cup victory.

Shankly was leaving the club, there was a widespread feeling of disbelief. When asked years later how he felt on that fateful day, Shankly replied: *'It was the most difficult thing in the world, when I went to tell the chairman. It was like walking to the electric chair. That's the way I felt.'* He revealed in his autobiography that he had been thinking about it for over a year. He had always spent an incredible amount of time away from home, checking on players and opponents, or going to be guest of honour at some social function. Shankly always gave 100 per cent effort to whatever task he set himself and he was mentally tired. His wife Nessie said it was for her that he brought his football management career to a close: *'Last year I asked him to think about retirement and it's for me he has announced it. Bill's as fit as a fiddle, but you can be fit and still be tired. He gives so much of himself to the game.'* It wasn't just the pressure of football that was taking its toll on Shankly, but some of the activities to which he often gave himself willingly that the media knew little of. *'Bill would often make visits to the local children's hospital at Alder Hey'*, said Nessie. *'Some of the children were terminally ill and when he arrived home in the evening after visiting them he would break down in tears. It was because he didn't have the ability to make them better. I did suggest to him that perhaps he should think about taking a break from his hospital visits, and he would get angry and say "I've said I'll visit the children and I'll go on visiting them" and that was that.'*

Peter Robinson was Liverpool's club secretary at the time and had built up a close working relationship with Shankly. Robinson, who is now the club's chief executive, revealed that he had spent the summer trying to get Shankly to change his mind, but once his decision was made, there was no going back. *'The board were desperate for him to stay in any capacity'*, remembers Robinson. *'He could have any job he wanted. He said he was tired and needed a rest, so we said he could come in one day a week if he wanted. But Bill was adamant and if I couldn't persuade him no one else could.'* Former Liverpool manager Joe Fagan, who worked with Shankly from day one of his arrival in 1959, said that neither himself nor Bob Paisley, who were Shankly's two closest members of the backroom staff at the club, ever found out why he wanted to go.

Bill Shankly announces his retirement on 12 July 1974. *'It was the most difficult thing in the world when I went to tell the chairman. It was like walking to the electric chair. That's the way I felt'* explained Shankly.

Although he had retired from professional football Shankly could still not get enough of the game and he kept up his daily training schedule, often at Liverpool's training ground at Melwood. They continued to worship the former Liverpool boss and if he was spotted at Anfield the chant would go up: 'Shankly, Shankly, Shankly'. If he was at Goodison Park, the home of arch-rivals Everton, he would even get an ovation there. It was the same if he

Opposite: Bill Shankly OBE with his wife Nessie, 1974.

Left: Peter Robinson, the Liverpool club secretary during the Shankly era and later the club's chief executive. He tried hard to keep Shankly at Liverpool.

attempted to go shopping with Nessie in Liverpool city centre. Nessie recalls: *'Bill refused to walk past anyone if they stopped to say hello to him. He would stop and chat. When we were out shopping in Liverpool, we would always return empty-handed because Bill has spent the entire afternoon chatting to people. In the end we had to go to Manchester to do the shopping.'*

Sunday afternoon was the highlight of the week for Shankly. He would play in a match organised by local dads with their children. Dressed in his Liverpool tracksuit, it was the FA Cup final at Wembley all over again to Shankly, as he put every ounce of effort into making sure his side won.

Inevitably Shankly's training sessions at Melwood did lead to a certain amount of angst. The other professionals in the Liverpool squad found it hard to get out of the habit of referring to Shankly as 'boss'. Liverpool wanted Paisley to be quickly accepted by the squad as the new manager and friction between the club and Shankly did develop. Shankly felt he was unwanted and took to watching the club's home games from different sections of the ground, rather than the director's box. He even took up a fan's suggestion that he should come into the Kop. Recalling this

occasion, Shankly said: '*I went into the Kop, not out of bravado, but because I was their man. Not only the Kop, the Anfield Road, the Paddock, the Kemlyn Road, the whole of Anfield.*' Once news spread that Shankly was in among them, the chant went up 'Shankly is our king, Shankly is our king' from a jubilant Kop. Shankly continued to support his beloved Liverpool, but there was now a distance between himself and the club. He was in Rome for Liverpool's historic first European Cup victory in 1977, and when asked was he envious of Paisley's success, he replied: '*Too bloody right I am.*'

It seemed to everyone that the super-fit Shankly was incapable of even suffering a day's illness. He had always joked: '*When I die, I*

Bill Shankly shakes hands with Ray Clemence before an Anfield testimonial game.

Shankly and Paisley embrace at Anfield after the Scot had handed over the managerial reigns to Paisley.

want people to walk past the coffin and say, "Christ there lies a fit man!"'
There was, therefore, a feeling of widespread disbelief throughout
the football world when the news was relayed that Shankly had
suffered a heart attack. He was rushed to hospital and it was
thought that he was over the worst when a few days later his
condition deteriorated again.

Bill Shankly died on 29 September 1981.

The staff and players of Liverpool Football Club, past and present,
were heartbroken. Tommy Smith had had his run-ins over the years
with the man he now refers to as a soccer god, but along with most
of the Liverpool players from the Shankly era, he thought the world
of the man. Bill Shankly had friends everywhere, not just those who
were involved in the game, but the thousands he had shown
kindness and encouragement to throughout the years. Today,
twenty-three years after his death, he remains a football icon. In
death, as in life, the spirit of Shankly dominates Liverpool Football
Club. To a great many people on Merseyside and elsewhere, Shankly
was the only real hero they will ever have in their lives. A smile
inevitably comes to their faces, and tears to their eyes, when former
players and Liverpool fans talk about Shankly. To the many
thousands who support the club, from near and afar, they are just
grateful that they were around during the Shankly years.

13

HE MADE THE PEOPLE HAPPY

Kevin Keegan was recently quoted as saying: *'Liverpool should be playing in the Shankly Stadium now. There shouldn't just be a set of gates named after him.'* As time goes on, the Shankly legend grows stronger, not just with the Liverpool supporters past and present, but with his former players as well. Shankly's quips and post-match remarks are now repeated on a daily basis, and are even used to form questions on the 'who said this' section of television programmes such as *University Challenge.* No other football manager, past or present, is regarded with such esteem. Other managers have won numerous trophies, such as the great Sir Matt Busby at Manchester United and Shankly's magnificent successor at Liverpool, Bob Paisley. Both were also highly crucial figures, like Shankly, in building up their respective clubs into the world-famous empires they are today. But when was the last time you heard them quoted, or saw their former players close to tears when recounting some anecdote about them? The Shankly legend, and the stories about him, will continue to be told and retold because the man was unique. Writing in 1980 when his former manager was still alive, Tommy Smith, who probably had more bust-ups with Shankly than any other Liverpool players, said: *'I still say anyone who comes into contact with Bill Shankly comes out a better person. You mightn't like him, you might think he's a bloody nuisance, but I'm grateful for all he taught me.'* Today Tommy's admiration for

Shankly's 'Bootroom boys'. From left to right, back row: Ronnie Moran, Bob Paisley, Joe Fagan. Front row: Roy Evans, Tom Saunders, John Bennison. Along with Reuben Bennett they sat with Shankly for many hours in the hallowed bootroom at Anfield and formulated Liverpool's plan to take over the football world.

Shankly has grown stronger with each passing year and he never tires of talking about the man.

Particularly prevalent in the memories of Shankly's former players is the kindness and concern that their former boss showed to the Liverpool fans. At away games, he'd tell his team as they drove through the fans near the ground: *'See them, boys, don't let them down. Some of them can't afford it, yet they're still here to support you.'* Ray Clemence described the occasions when Shankly would bail out Reds fans who'd arrived in London with no train tickets: *'We used to go down on the train to play London sides. One or two Scousers would get on the train and not buy tickets. Invariably they'd get caught at the other end. Shanks, on many occasions, would go up to the ticket master and pay for those fans. They were in trouble, but he'd go and pay for them to get them out of trouble.'* Fans also recalled Shankly's concern for their fellow

Bill Shankly sits in the director's box at Anfield with Bob Paisley and Joe Fagan to watch Liverpool play Manchester United. A young Martin Edwards is also in the picture.

Liverpool supporters. One Liverpool fan said of a mid-1960s away game at Southampton: '*I watched as the Liverpool team coach pulled up outside the ground. As the players stepped off the coach and made their way into the players' entrance, Shanks walked over to a couple of Liverpool kids and asked them if they had had something to eat. He then took out his wallet and gave them a few pound notes. "Don't let me down, boys. Straight over to the café and get yourselves a nice warm meal", he told them. I watched as they immediately obeyed his orders. Gestures such as this were typical of the man.*'

The idea that Bill Shankly, however, was some kind of saintly figure who never upset people would be totally misleading. Numerous football journalists, as well as Shankly's players, would often find themselves on the receiving end of a tongue lashing from the idiosyncratic Scot if he thought they deserved it. Colin Wood of the *Daily Mail* once said: '*Working with Shankly was often like treading through a minefield. One false step and the explosion could blow you into little pieces. But then the warmth, the quick smile that told you that you were forgiven, and the invitation to a cup of tea put you back together again.*' Wood claimed that Shankly only ever held a grudge against one reporter, the journalist who left Wembley during extra time and missed Liverpool's famous victory over Leeds in the 1965 FA Cup final. That was sacrilege to Shankly. In general, he didn't bear a grudge against any of his players who dared to argue with him either. He once admitted that he didn't care if a player didn't like him: *'I deal with everybody as I think fit. Whether they like it or whether they don't, doesn't make any difference to me.'* Some at Anfield didn't appreciate Shankly's style, particularly during his early days there. Former international footballer and sports journalist Ivor Broadis once remarked: *'I remember someone at Liverpool saying Bill could be an awkward bugger. This other chap replied "Aye, if Bill wasn't an awkward bugger, we'd still be in the Second Division".'*

Shankly could certainly be scathing at times, particularly if any of his players reported themselves injured. *'Get that poof bandage off your leg!'* he was alleged to have told one of his team who turned up at Melwood with his leg strapped up. *'But Boss, my leg...' 'Your leg!'*, Shankly exploded. *'Your leg! That's Liverpool's leg. What do you mean, your leg!'* Injured players would quite often be sent to Coventry by Shankly. Once the injury had cleared up, Shankly would pass the time of day again with them. Tommy Smith once said that the way you were treated by Shankly when injured was quite comical: *'You would be lying on the treatment table and Bob Paisley might be giving you some treatment. Shankly would come in and ignore you, but say to Bob, "How is Smithy's leg?" I'd reply "Tell Mr Shankly that Smith's leg isn't too good." Still ignoring me, Shanks would say "Will he be fit for Saturday?" Bob would convey the question to me and I'd say "Tell Mr Shankly that Smith doesn't know yet." This is the way it would carry on, with Shanks not asking me a direct question but talking through Bob.'* An injured player was no use to Liverpool Football Club, and right from the start Shankly expected his players to be as fanatical as him in their desire to take Liverpool to the top. He was known to have contacted golf clubs on Merseyside to check if any of his players were disobeying his request that they shouldn't participate in the sport. In Shankly's opinion, golf wasn't beneficial to certain parts of the human anatomy. And it was the same when it came to alcohol. Shankly didn't mind his players having the odd beer, but if they

The Kop salutes Bill Shankly.

overstepped the mark he would come down hard on them. *'Every player that comes here from the first day is being watched. We read them like a book. If he thinks that nobody is watching him, he's got a surprise coming'*, Shankly once declared. On one famous occasion, Shankly is reputed to have entered a Liverpool city centre club and dragged a player out by his hair, after the Liverpool manager had received reports that the player had been overdoing his night-clubbing activities.

Bill Shankly was undoubtedly totally selfless in his determination to turn Liverpool into a great club. Bob Paisley once said: *'One man transformed Liverpool from a run-of-the-mill Second Division team into the greatest club in the world. That man, of course, was Bill Shankly. His philosophy was simple: If you are going to play football, you play to win. While he was the making of Liverpool, there is no doubt that Anfield was the making of Bill Shankly. His character, his own enthusiasm, his will to win were so infectious.'* When asked what made Shankly so special as a manager, many of his former players cite his incredible ability to motivate them on the field of play. *'I was a big lad, but when the boss finished with me, I felt even bigger. Having arrived from Scotland with a "will I make it?" feeling and perhaps lacking in confidence, Shanks made a fantastic difference to my game'*, recalls former Liverpool skipper Ron Yeats. Alec Lindsay also felt the same about Shankly motivating him into becoming a better player: *'He got me working at my game, at my fitness, and he worked on my confidence. I was tried at left-back and never looked back.'* FA Cup final hero Gerry Byrne was actually on the transfer list when Shankly arrived at the club: *'I was in the reserves and seriously thinking about leaving when there was a change in manager and Bill Shankly came. Bill had confidence in me and I always tried never to let him down. That's one of the reasons why I was determined to stay on in the FA Cup final at Wembley. I would have done it just for him.'* Player after player expresses the same sentiments about Shankly's motivational abilities. Soccer legend Sir Tom Finney also noted that Shankly, Finney's former teammate at Preston, was an expert at getting the best out of players: *'He got ordinary players performing beyond their capabilities, make them believe that they were better than even they thought.'*

Shankly himself, however, believed that simply putting on the red shirt of Liverpool was enough motivation in itself. *'Fire in your belly comes from pride and passion in wearing the red shirt'*, he would often proclaim. During the Shankly era, just the first sight of Anfield from their team coach would often strike the fear of God into most opposition players. *'We don't need to motivate players'*, Shankly said, *'because each of them is responsible for the performance of the team as a whole. We aren't expecting a player to win a game by himself. We share out the worries. The status of Liverpool's players keeps them motivated.'* Liverpool's ability to 'share out the worries' as Shankly described it, enabled him to build two great teams, even though the teams weren't each comprised of eleven outstanding players. The players who weren't considered to be top-notch fitted in because of the great players in their team. Shankly, though he would be loathe to admit it – each of his players being described by him as the best player in that position in the world – did have his share of ordinary players. But within the framework of the Liverpool team they became competent until they gelled together into a very effective whole.

Many of Shankly's players were never really a success when tried at international level but were outstanding when representing Liverpool. The Leeds, Manchester United and Celtic teams of the 1960s also had their share of competent but not outstanding players. Yet all of these teams, like Shankly's Liverpool, achieved much success. Perhaps if Shankly could have been persuaded to give up his beloved Liverpool and take over a Scotland team (which could boast such outstanding world-class players as Law, Bremner, Baxter and Mackay), with his phenomenal powers of motivation, they, not England, might have been the first British side to win a World Cup. *'He mayn't have had any degrees in psychology, but he was the best brain-washer I've ever encountered – he used to make players feel like giants, and opponents almost like pygmies!'* declared Bob Paisley when asked about Shankly's ability to psyche his team up before a game.

Towards the end of 1997, a bronze figure of Bill Shankly in messianic pose, standing ten feet tall, was unveiled at Anfield. The statue stands in the shadow of the Kop and is made from red Scottish granite. Many of his former players were present for the ceremony. Shankly's great friend and former teammate Tommy Docherty told waiting reporters: *'Bill Shankly was fantastic, a great man and a great character and a man very much of the people. He'll never be forgotten anywhere in the world, but especially at Anfield where they absolutely idolise him. Shankly thought just as much of the supporters as well. They are fantastic supporters.'*

The inscription on the base of the statue says simply 'Bill Shankly 1913-1981 – He made the People Happy'.

The honour of unveiling the statue was given to Shankly's captain from the 1960s, Ron Yeats, who had once said of Shankly: *'He took Liverpool from nothing, and perhaps more difficult, he kept the club on the*

Liverpool sculptor Tom Murphy's bronze statue of Bill Shankly is unveiled at
Anfield in 1997. Members of his great 1960s team pay their respects. From left
to right: Roger Hunt, Tommy Lawrence, Chris Lawler, Peter Thompson, Ron
Yeats, Willie Stevenson, Ian Callaghan and Gerry Byrne. The presence of
Shankly will loom large over Anfield for many years to come.

rails. A lot of clubs come up but they don't manage to keep it going.' Perhaps
the most fitting tribute to Shankly came from one of his beloved
Anfield faithful, who said: *'Bill Shankly gave his life to Liverpool
Football Club. He never made much money from the game, but he died a
much richer man than some of the second-rate managers who now reside in
country mansions will ever be.'*

14

THE GREAT MOTIVATOR

The secret of Shankly's managerial success owed a great deal to his ability to motivate. Practically every player who played under Shankly, whether it was in the Third Division at Carlisle and Workington, or in the First Division with Liverpool, claims that Shankly's ability to motivate was phenomenal. Every player that Shankly signed was told the same message: you're going to become a great player. Ron Yeats, recalling his initial period at Liverpool, once said: *'I was a big lad, but when the Boss had finished even I felt bigger – I could have reached the roof of the Kop. To him we were each the best player in our respective positions in the history of the game and there wasn't a team in the world that could live with us – or so he had us believe. Having arrived from Scotland with a "will I make it?" feeling and perhaps lacking in confidence, he made a fantastic difference to my game. Even I could sense the improvement in my play.'*

Shankly was also a master at pinpointing a player's strong points and weaknesses. Full-back Alec Lindsay was initially overawed when he first arrived at Liverpool from Bury and his confidence in his playing ability began to wane. Lindsay recalls that: *'I was signed from Bury as a midfield player, but at first couldn't settle in. I was stripping alongside Roger Hunt and Peter Thompson and asking myself how the hell I had got there. I lost all my confidence and felt really down. But Shankly wasn't having any of that for long. He got me working at my game, at my*

Bill Shankly photographed on the team bus during Liverpool's triumphant homecoming tour after their 1974 FA Cup victory over Newcastle.

fitness, and he worked at my confidence. Then, as I had played in the left side of defence on occasion at Bury, I was tried on the left-hand side of the back four – and I never looked back.' Lindsay went on to become an international player at this position.

Shankly also had the ability to spot the players who suffered from pre-match nerves and would quickly put them at their ease with just a few simple words. Emlyn Hughes recalled: *'I've seen players sitting in the dressing room quaking with nerves. They could hear the roar of the crowd through the dressing room walls, they knew what a big job was in front of them, and they would just go to pieces. But then in walks Shanks, and before the player knows, he's feeling tremendous, like a new man. Once Shanks had turned on his "magic" you'd go out and face any opposition – simply because, I think, you believe what Shanks said. Sometimes it might have been outrageous, but usually it was just sound, simple sense.'*

To Shankly the game and how to play it was simplicity itself. He never tried to complicate things in either training or playing and he scorned the new phraseology of modern-day football. But in many ways, the tactics that the Shankly teams of the 1960s and 70s employed were ahead of their time. He was probably the first manager to introduce a cover defender alongside the centre half; which, in the successful 1960s team, tended to be Tommy Smith playing alongside Ron Yeats. Indeed, Shankly was reported to have explained the new role that he wanted Smith to play by telling him to think of himself as Ron Yeats' right leg! Shankly also coached his defenders to push up and his forwards to take up a midfield role when the opposition had the ball. This system reduced the space available to the opposition and would deny them time to play the ball. It was a system that most teams found hard to come to terms with and was the basis of much of Liverpool's success. To play this system, however, Shankly's teams had to be superbly fit and Shankly would at times drive his players on relentlessly until the desired level of fitness was attained. Shankly would never ask his players to attempt a training activity that he would not have been able to accomplish himself during his playing days and when it came to five-a-side games, he demanded that his players did not hold back with the tackles on him as he played alongside them. It was also important to him that his players were given a lot of ball work in training. *'Joe Davies doesn't run around the snooker table'* he once exclaimed, as he recalled the training methods of some clubs, who would simply run players around the playing area day after day with not a sight of the ball until match day. Preseason road running at Anfield was also abolished by Shankly, who commented: *'You don't play on tarmac, you play on grass.'* Shankly also changed the way that the youth players at Anfield were treated. Chris Lawler was a ground staff boy at Anfield when Shankly arrived in 1959. His main tasks were to sweep the changing rooms and clean the first team players' boots. *'That's no good for you, you're going to be footballers'* Shankly told Lawler and the other ground staff teenagers. From then on the ground staff boys trained with the first team and reserve players and only carried out their cleaning duties when the day's training was over.

Perhaps the most well known of Shankly's motivational tactics was the way in which he vilified the opposition. Interviewed by the *Liverpool Echo* in the 1970s Bob Paisley recalled Shankly's pre-match team talks: '*His personality was overwhelming. It was this terrific personality, his passion for the game, which enabled him to lift players. He did it by personality, not by tactical talks. He didn't have tactical talks at Anfield as most people understand them. Your opponents couldn't play. His favourite word was 'rubbish'. He would tell the Liverpool players that their opponents were rubbish and they were the greatest. It may sound silly, but it worked with Bill Shankly because of his personality. He made his players believe.*'

Tom Saunders, who was Youth Development Officer at Anfield during the Shankly years, was also privy to some of Shankly's pre-match talks and recalled one occasion when football was the last topic on the agenda: '*The players waited for their instructions and Shankly began to speak and continued for some fifteen minutes. Not about the opposition or even football. Oh no! Boxing was the sole subject for a quarter of an hour. He then switched to football but quickly brought the proceedings to a halt. "Don't let's waste time! That bloody lot can't play at all." With that, the team talk was rapidly brought to a close.*' But Saunders had no doubts that Shankly's constant rubbishing of the opposition was a shrewd Shankly tactic that gave the Liverpool players an aura of invincibility that was worth a good start. On the odd occasion, however, Shankly would praise the opposition but once again it would be part of his ploy to boost his own players' self-esteem. Bob Paisley recalled Shankly praising one of their European opponents, Anderlecht, who boasted Belgian internationals in their team: '*Before the game, in the dressing room, Bill talked to the lads. He said "You've read about Anderlecht having all these internationals and how good they are. Forget it. They can't play. They're rubbish. I've seen them and I'm telling you. You'll murder them, so get out there and do it." The boys went out there and murdered them. They won 3-0. And after the game, Bill burst into the dressing room and said "Boys, you've just beaten the greatest team in Europe."*' Because of the strength of his personality Shankly could

Bill Shankly displays the FA Charity Shield at Wembley, 1974.

tell his players one thing and then totally contradict what he had told them yet, somehow, they accepted it without question.

Another key factor in Shankly's managerial success was the incredible amount of time he invested in the game. Shankly would travel the length and breadth of Britain watching matches in his endless search for new talent. During his early days at Liverpool, he was known to have personally checked on over thirty centre halves before deciding to sign Ron Yeats. Although Shankly liked nothing

Brian Clough and Bill Shankly lead out their Leeds and Liverpool sides at Wembley, 1974.

better than to be at home with his feet up watching television, his pursuit of success for Liverpool meant that he did not often get the chance to relax. Tommy Docherty, aware of the long hours that Shankly spent watching football around the country once remarked: *'If he'd been paid overtime, he'd have been a millionaire.'* But to Shankly the long hours were all part of the job as he acknowledged in his autobiography: *'I've been a slave to football. It follows you home, it follows you everywhere, and eats into your family life. But every working man misses out on some things because of his job.'* To Shankly it was a price he was prepared to pay in his relentless drive to make Liverpool FC the greatest team in the land.

15

WIT AND WISDOM

The quotations and anecdotes involving Bill Shankly are legendary and could fill a book on their own. Here is a selection of some of the most memorable ones.

'Football is not a matter of life and death; it's much more important than that.'

'A lot of football success is in the mind. You must believe you are the best and then make sure you are. In my time at Liverpool, we always said we had the best two teams on Merseyside: Liverpool and Liverpool Reserves.'

'If you are first, you are first. If you are second, you are nothing.'

'The trouble with football referees is that they know the rules but they do not know the game.'

'Of course I didn't take my wife to see Rochdale as an anniversary present. It was her birthday. Would I have got married during the football season? And anyway, it wasn't Rochdale, it was Rochdale Reserves.'

To a reporter in the 1960s: *'Yes, Roger Hunt misses a few, but he gets in the right place to miss them.'*

Shankly liked to tell the following story about the 1966 Everton *v.* Sheffield Wednesday FA Cup final: *'Princess Margaret asked Everton captain, Brian Labone: "Mr Labone, where is Everton?" Labone answered "In Liverpool, Ma'am." To which Princess Margaret replied, "Of course, we had your first team here last year."'*

After signing Scottish giant, Ron Yeats, Shankly remarked: *'With him in defence, we could play Arthur Askey in goal.'*

After a hard fought 1-1 result, Shankly's post-match comment was: *'The best side drew.'*

When Liverpool were held to a 0-0 draw at Anfield, he commented: *'What can you do, playing against eleven goalposts?'*

Shankly once told a journalist who made the mistake of criticising his team selection: *'Laddie, I never drop players, I only make changes.'*

Explaining the 'This is Anfield' plaque in the Liverpool tunnel: *'It reminds our players where they are… and it warns the opposition.'*

To Shankly there was no finer stadium than Anfield and he once remarked on the pitch: *'It's great grass at Anfield, professional grass.'*

After the erection of a new stand at Anfield in 1971: *'The ground is now fit for our great team and our wonderful supporters.'*

After hearing that Celtic's Lou Macari had turned down Liverpool in favour of Manchester United, he covered his obvious dejection by telling his squad: *'He couldn't play anyway. I only wanted him for the reserve team.'*

Shankly was reputed to be the only manager of an English club at the famous Celtic *v.* Inter Milan European Cup final in Portugal in 1967. After Celtic became the first British team to win the trophy, he told his friend Jock Stein: *'John you're immortal now. Mind you, Liverpool would have beaten that lot!'*

Jock Stein, himself a noted wit, once said: *'I don't believe everything Bill tells me about his players. Had they been that good, they'd not only have won the European Cup, but the Ryder Cup, the Boat Race and even the Grand National!'*

On one of Liverpool's numerous European trips, he was filling in the hotel registration form, writing 'football' under 'occupation' and 'Anfield' under 'address'. *'But sir'*, protested the receptionist, *'you need to fill in where you live.'* *'Lady'*, replied Shankly, *'in Liverpool there is only one address that matters and that is where I live.'*

Negotiating a transfer deal in his office, he was distracted by the noise of reporters having a kick about in the car park to pass time before the announcement. *'What the hell!'* he roared, *'They can't play football. Bob, Reuben, Joe, Ronnie... get the strips and we'll play them five-a-side!'*

During another five-a-side match at Melwood, Shankly scored a goal. When the other players insisted it was offside, he turned to Chris Lawler, one of the quietest members in the squad. *'Was it a goal?'* he demanded, *'Was I offside?'* *'Yes, boss you were'*, Lawler replied. Shankly looked at him in utter disbelief: *'Chris, you've been here for four years and have never said a word and when you do it's a bloody lie!'*

Attending the funeral of Everton legend Dixie Dean, Shankly was amazed by the size of the crowd outside St James' church. Shaking his head in wonderment, he remarked: *'I know this is a sad occasion but I think that Dixie would have been amazed to know that even in death he could draw a bigger crowd than Everton can on a Saturday afternoon.'*

When it was put to him that he did not have the experience of playing in an Everton v. Liverpool derby match, unlike Everton manager Billy Bingham, he replied: *'Nonsense! I've kicked every ball, headed out every cross. I once scored a hat-trick; one was lucky but the others were great goals.'*

After the sensational defeat of Everton in the 1971 Cup semi-final he commented: *'Sickness would not have kept me away from this one. If I'd been dead, I would have had them bring the casket to the ground, prop it up in the stands and put a hole in the lid.'*

During the 1960s, when Liverpool and Everton rivalry was intense, Shankly still found time to ring up Everton's Alan Ball, a player he greatly admired, to talk football. Alan Ball once remarked: *'Shankly was very special. The greatness of the man was the fact that he wasn't frightened to give praise, even if it was to the so-called worst enemy.'*

Shankly was famed for his telephone calls to other managers. Bill Nicholson, the great Spurs manager, recalls a Sunday morning call: *'After the usual hellos, I mentioned Liverpool's 2-0 defeat the previous day. Quick as a flash, Bill growled, 'No, No Billy... we murdered them, we were all over them. The first wasn't a goal at all and the second, well, you've never seen anything like it.'*

Don Revie regularly received a Sunday morning call. Each followed the same ritual, with Shankly eulogising over his Liverpool players. Every player would be praised, including the substitute who would have contributed to the victory even if he had not played. To Shankly every player in that red strip had everything: a right foot, left foot, tackling, heading and stamina. No player had a weakness, they were each the best player, position for position, in the world. When Revie managed to get in a mention of one of his own players, Shankly would just say *'a fair player, nae bad'*, leaving Revie wondering how Leeds ever managed to win a match with no great players, not even good ones for all that Bill would admit to.

Barry Farrell, the photographer, once asked Shankly whether he thought Brian Clough's outspokenness was doing him a disservice. *'Laddie'*, retorted an annoyed Shankly, *'that man scored some 200 goals in 270 matches – an incredible record – and he has won cup after cup as a manager. When he talks, pin back your ears.'*

Football and boxing were his two great loves but football always came first. Alan Rudkin offered Shankly tickets for his title fight with Walter McGovern, which were accepted enthusiastically. However, on the morning of the fight Rudkin received a telephone call: *'Alan, I'm sorry but I can't make it. There's a schoolboy match I want to see.'*

Rudkin also remembered hosting a meeting of Liverpool fans from London at Anfield. Shankly entered the room and turned to one awestruck fan: *'Where are you from?'* Nervously the boy answered: *'I'm a Liverpool fan from London.'* Shankly responded: *'Well, laddie… what's it like to be in heaven?'*

Right up until his last day with Liverpool, Shankly was full of wit and humour. Just before his retirement was announced, television crews had arrived and began switching on the lights. *'Hold it a minute'*, he called out, *'John Wayne hasn't arrived yet.'*

Having made his retirement speech, he left to sign Ray Kennedy from Arsenal with a parting comment: *'There'll not be many days like this.'*

Bill Shankly, still a Liverpool icon thirty years after he retired as manager.

16

A LIFETIME'S RECORD

Shankly's Record as a Player

Cronberry Juniors
Scottish Junior League: 1930–32

Carlisle United, Third Division (North)
Joined: July 1932
Debut: 31 December 1932 *v.* Rochdale
Appeared in 16 league games

Preston North End, Second Division
Joined: July 1933
Debut: 9 December 1933 *v.* Hull City
First league goal: 2 February 1938 *v.* Liverpool
Final game: March 19, 1949 *v.* Sunderland
League appearances: 297
Goals: 13 league goals (8 penalties)
Honours: 1933–34 Second Division Runners-up
1936–37 FA Cup Runners-up
1937–38 FA Cup Winners

International Record for Scotland
1938 *v.* England
1939 *v.* England
1939 *v.* Wales
1939 *v.* Northern Ireland
1939 *v.* Hungary

Wartime Honours

Seven wartime international caps
1940/41 Played for Preston North End when they won the North Regional
League Championship
1940/41 Played for Preston in their successful wartime League Cup final
victory over Arsenal. Preston won after a replay
Shankly created a football league record when he played 43 successive FA
Cup ties for one club, Preston North End
RAF representative honours in football and boxing

Bill Shankly leads Liverpool out at Wembley before the 1971 FA Cup final
against Arsenal.

Shankly's Managerial Career

Carlisle United
Joined March 1949, first game in charge 9 April

Season	Played	Won	Drew	Lost	Final League Position
1948/49	7	1	4	2	15th Third Division (North)
1949/50	42	16	15	11	9th Third Division (North)
1950/51	46	25	12	9	3rd Third Division (North)

Grimsby Town
Joined July 1951

Season	Played	Won	Drew	Lost	Final League Position
1951/52	46	29	8	9	2nd Third Division (North)
1952/53	47	22	9	15	5th Third Division (North)
1953/54★	26	11	4	11	–

★Shankly resigned on 2 January 1954

Workington
Became manager 6 January 1954

Season	Played	Won	Drew	Lost	Final League Position
1953/54	20	8	6	6	18th Third Division (North)
1954/55	46	18	14	14	8th Third Division (North)
1955/56★	19	9	3	7	–

★Shankly resigned on 15 November 1955

Huddersfield Town
Joined 10 December 1955, became manager 5 November 1956

Season	Played	Won	Drew	Lost	Final League Position
1956/57	26	11	4	11	12th Second Division
1957/58	42	14	16	12	9th Second Division
1958/59	42	16	8	18	14th Second Division
1959/60★	19	8	5	6	–

★Shankly resigned on 1 December 1959

Liverpool

Joined December 1959, first game in charge 19 December

Season	Played	Won	Drew	Lost	Final League Position
1959/60	21	11	5	5	3rd Second Division
1960/61	42	21	10	11	3rd Second Division
1961/62	42	27	8	7	1st Second Division
1962/63	42	17	10	15	8th First Division
1963/64	42	26	5	11	1st First Division
1964/65	42	17	10	15	7th First Division
1965/66	42	26	9	7	1st First Division
1966/67	42	19	13	10	5th First Division
1967/68	42	22	11	9	3rd First Division
1968/69	42	25	11	6	2nd First Division
1969/70	42	20	11	11	5th First Division
1970/71	42	17	17	8	5th First Division
1971/72	42	24	9	9	3rd First Division
1972/73	42	25	10	7	1st First Division
1973/74	42	22	13	7	2nd First Division

Honours as Liverpool Manager

1961/62	Second Division Champions
1962/63	FA Cup semi-finalists
1963/64	First Division Champions
1964/65	FA Cup winners
	European Cup semi-finalists
1965/66	First Division Champions
	European Cup Winners' Cup runners-up
1970/71	FA Cup runners-up
	European Cup Winners' Cup semi-finalists
1972/73	First Division Champions
	UEFA Cup winners
	Manager Of The Year trophy
1973/74	FA Cup winners

The Liverpool First Division title-winning squad, 1963/64.

The Shankly Signings

With the possible exception of Kevin Keegan and Larry Lloyd, all of the Shankly signings were resold with their best playing years well behind them. Yet he still managed to show a net profit of well over half a million pounds (still a substantial sum in the 1970s). The lessons he learnt running a tight financial ship during his formative managerial years at Carlisle, Grimsby and Workington stayed with him for the rest of his career. Although not afraid to splash out on players when the situation demanded it, the profit figures show what a shrewd financial brain Shankly had.

1960   Bought: Sammy Reid, (Winger) £8,000 from Motherwell

1960   Bought: Kevin Lewis, (Winger) £13,000 from Sheffield United
1963   Sold to Huddersfield Town for £18,000

1960   Bought: Gordon Milne, (Midfield) £16,000 from Preston
1967   Sold to Blackpool for £30,000

1961   Bought: Ian St John, (Striker) £37,500 from Motherwell
1971   Sold to Coventry City for no fee

1961   Bought: Ron Yeats, (Centre half) £30,000 from Dundee United
1971   Sold to Tranmere Rovers for no fee

1961   Bought: Jim Furnell, (Goalkeeper) £18,000 from Burnley
1964   Sold to Arsenal for £15,000

1962   Bought: Willie Stevenson, (Midfield) £20,000 from Rangers
1968   Sold to Stoke City for £48,000

1963   Bought: Peter Thompson, (Winger) £32,000 from Preston North End
1974   Sold to Bolton Wanderers for £18,000

1964   Bought: Geoff Strong, (Utility) £40,000 from Arsenal
1970   Sold to Coventry City for £30,000

1964   Bought: Phil Chisnall, (Striker) £24,000 from Manchester United
1967   Sold to Southend United for £12,000

1965   Bought: John Ogston, (Goalkeeper) £10,000 from Aberdeen
1968   Sold to Doncaster Rovers for £2,500

1966   Bought: Stuart Mason, (Full-back) £20,000 from Wrexham
1968   Sold to Wrexham for no fee

1966   Bought: Peter Wall, (Full-back) £6,000 from Wrexham
1970   Sold to Crystal Palace for £35,000

1966   Bought: Dave Wilson (Winger) £20,000 from Preston North End
1968   Sold to Preston North End for £4,000

1966   Bought: Emlyn Hughes (Defence/Midfield) £65,000 from Blackpool
1979   Sold to Wolverhampton Wanderers for £90,000

1967   Bought: Tony Hateley (Striker) £96,000 from Chelsea
1969   Sold to Coventry City for £80,000

1968   Bought: Alun Evans (Striker) £100,000 from Wolverhampton Wanderers
1972   Sold to Aston Villa for £70,000

1968   Bought: Ray Clemence, (Goalkeeper) £18,000 from Scunthorpe
1981   Sold to Tottenham Hotspur for £300,000

1969   Bought: Alec Lindsay, (Full-back) £68,000 from Bury
1977   Sold to Stoke City for £20,000

1969   Bought: Larry Lloyd, (Centre half) £50,000 from Bristol Rovers
1974   Sold to Coventry City £225,000

1970   Bought: Jack Whitham, (Striker) £57,000 from Sheffield Wednesday
1974   Sold to Cardiff City for no fee

1970   Bought: Steve Heighway, (Winger) no fee from Skelmersdale
1981   Sold to Minnesota Kicks for no fee

1970   Bought: John Toshack, (Striker) £110,000 from Cardiff City
1978   Sold to Swansea City for no fee

1971   Bought: Kevin Keegan, (Striker) £35,000 from Scunthorpe
1977   Sold to SV Hamburg for £500,000

1972   Bought: Trevor Storton (Centre half) £25,000 from Tranmere Rovers
1974   Sold to Chester City for £18,000

1972   Bought: Frank Lane (Goalkeeper) £15,000 from Tranmere Rovers
1975   Sold to Notts County for no fee

1972   Bought: Peter Cormack, (Midfield) £110,000 from Nottingham Forest
1976   Sold to Bristol City for £50,000

1973   Bought: Alan Waddle, (Striker) £40,000 from Halifax Town
1977   Sold to Leicester City for £45,000

1974   Bought: Ray Kennedy (Striker/Midfield) £200,000 from Arsenal
1982   Sold to Swansea City for £160,000

The Shankly Players 1959-1974

The following is a full list of the players who appeared for Liverpool during the Shankl[
era at Anfield, not including the Charity Shield.

A=Appearances
S=Substitutions
G=Goals

Player	League			FA Cup			L/Milk			Europe			Total		
	A	S	G	A	S	G	A	S	G	A	S	G	A	S	C
Alan A'Court	119	0	20	9	0	1	2	0	0	0	0	0	130	0	2
Alan Arnell	1	0	0	0	0	0	0	0	0	0	0	0	1	0	
Steve Arnold	1	0	0	0	0	0	0	0	0	0	0	0	1	0	
Alf Arrowsmith	43	4	20	6	0	4	0	0	0	1	0	0	50	4	2
Alan Banks	5	0	4	0	0	0	0	0	0	0	0	0	5	0	
Reg Blore	1	0	0	0	0	0	0	0	0	0	0	0	1	0	
Phil Boersma	52	6	11	7	3	1	2	2	2	9	5	6	70	16	2
Derek Brownbill	1	0	0	0	0	0	0	0	0	0	0	0	1	0	
Gerry Byrne	273	1	2	29	0	0	5	0	0	22	0	1	329	1	
Ian Callaghan	497	3	44	68	1	2	27	0	6	59	1	7	651	5	5
Bobby Campbell	14	0	1	0	0	0	0	0	0	0	0	0	14	0	
Willie Carlin	1	0	0	0	0	0	0	0	0	0	0	0	1	0	
Phil Chisnall	6	0	1	0	0	0	0	0	0	2	0	1	8	0	
Ray Clemence	180	0	0	24	0	0	20	0	0	32	0	0	256	0	
Peter Cormack	70	2	17	12	0	2	14	0	1	11	0	1	107	2	2
Alun Evans	77	2	21	9	2	3	7	0	2	11	2	7	104	6	3
Roy Evans	9	0	0	0	0	0	1	0	0	1	0	0	11	0	
Chris Fagan	1	0	0	0	0	0	0	0	0	0	0	0	1	0	
Phil Fearns	27	0	1	1	0	0	0	0	0	0	0	0	28	0	
Jim Furnell	28	0	0	0	0	0	0	0	0	0	0	0	28	0	
Bobby Graham	96	5	31	7	2	4	7	1	2	13	0	5	123	8	4
Brian Hall	93	14	8	15	1	3	7	1	1	17	5	2	132	21	1
Jimmy Harrower	34	0	10	3	0	1	3	0	0	0	0	0	40	0	1
Tony Hateley	42	0	17	7	0	8	2	0	0	5	0	3	56	0	2
Steve Heighway	142	3	20	19	0	4	19	0	5	27	0	4	207	3	3
Dave Hickson	54	0	32	4	0	0	3	0	1	0	0	0	61	0	3
Alan Hignett	1	0	0	0	0	0	0	0	0	0	0	0	1	0	
Emlyn Hughes	294	0	31	42	0	1	27	0	3	42	0	7	405	0	4
Roger Hunt	386	3	237	44	0	18	10	0	5	29	2	17	469	5	27
Alan Jones	5	0	0	0	0	0	0	0	0	0	0	0	5	0	
Kevin Keegan	219	0	34	16	0	8	15	0	6	18	0	4	167	0	5
Frank Lane	1	0	0	0	0	0	1	0	0	0	0	0	2	0	

layer	League			FA Cup			L/Milk			Europe			Total		
	A	S	G	A	S	G	A	S	G	A	S	G	A	S	G
hris Lawler	396	0	41	47	0	4	24	0	5	62	0	11	529	0	61
ommy Lawrence	306	0	0	42	0	0	6	0	0	33	0	0	387	0	0
ommy Leishman	107	0	6	9	0	0	3	0	1	0	0	0	119	0	7
evin Lewis	71	0	39	8	0	3	2	0	0	0	0	0	81	0	42
illy Liddell	12	0	1	0	0	0	0	0	0	0	0	0	12	0	1
lec Lindsay	136	2	9	20	0	1	16	0	0	25	0	3	197	2	13
oug Livermore	13	3	0	0	0	0	1	0	0	0	0	0	14	3	0
arry Lloyd	150	0	4	16	0	0	20	0	0	31	0	1	217	0	5
om Lowry	1	0	0	0	0	0	0	0	0	0	0	0	1	0	0
hn McLaughlin	38	2	2	4	0	1	3	0	0	8	0	0	53	2	3
mmy Melia	144	0	28	15	0	2	0	0	0	0	0	0	159	0	30
ordon Milne	234	2	18	27	0	1	0	0	0	16	0	0	277	2	19
ill Molyneux	86	0	1	5	0	0	3	0	0	0	0	0	94	0	1
onnie Moran	131	0	10	15	0	2	0	0	0	4	0	0	150	0	12
red Morris	1	0	0	0	0	0	0	0	0	0	0	0	1	0	0
hnny Morrissey	23	0	5	1	0	0	0	0	0	0	0	0	24	0	5
hn Ogston	1	0	0	0	0	0	0	0	0	0	0	0	1	0	0
eve Peplow	2	0	0	0	0	0	0	0	0	1	0	0	3	0	0
n Ross	42	6	2	9	1	1	3	0	0	5	2	1	59	9	4
ave Rylands	0	0	0	1	0	0	0	0	0	0	0	0	1	0	0
hn Sealey	1	0	1	0	0	0	0	0	0	0	0	0	1	0	1
ert Slater	99	0	0	9	0	0	3	0	0	0	0	0	111	0	0
ommy Smith	369	0	32	46	0	2	20	0	2	63	1	6	498	1	42
illie Stevenson	188	0	15	24	0	1	0	0	0	25	1	0	237	1	16
n St John	334	2	95	49	1	12	6	0	1	30	2	10	419	5	118
revor Storton	5	0	0	1	0	0	4	0	0	1	1	0	11	1	0
eoff Strong	150	5	29	23	0	1	4	0	0	16	0	2	193	5	32
obby Thompson	6	0	0	1	0	0	0	0	0	0	0	0	7	0	0
ax Thompson	1	0	0	0	0	0	0	0	0	0	1	0	1	1	0
eter Thompson	318	4	41	37	1	5	9	0	2	40	3	6	404	8	54
hil Thompson	47	3	0	11	0	0	4	1	0	4	2	0	66	6	0
hn Toshack	90	1	36	18	0	6	9	0	3	15	3	3	132	4	48
lan Waddle	11	5	1	2	0	0	3	0	0	0	1	0	16	6	1
eter Wall	31	0	0	6	0	0	2	0	0	3	0	0	42	0	0
ordon Wallace	19	1	3	0	0	0	0	0	0	1	0	2	20	1	5
hnny Wheeler	46	0	5	3	0	1	3	0	0	0	0	0	52	0	6
ick White	87	0	0	5	0	0	3	0	0	0	0	0	95	0	0
ck Whitham	15	0	7	0	0	0	1	0	0	0	0	0	16	0	7
ave Wilson	0	1	0	0	0	0	0	0	0	0	0	0	0	1	0
on Yeats	357	1	13	50	0	0	7	0	0	36	0	2	460	1	15

BIBLIOGRAPHY

Ian Callaghan and John Keith, *The Ian Callaghan Story,* Quartet Books, 1975.

Ronald Cowling, Martin Lawson & Bill Willcox, *The Carlisle United Story,* Lakeside Publications, 1974.

Eamon Dunphy, *A Strange Kind of Glory: Sir Matt Busby and Manchester United,* Heinemann, 1991.

Roddy Forsyth, *The Only Game: The Scots and World Football,* Mainstream Publishing Company, 1990.

Terry Frost, *Huddersfield Town: A Complete Record 1910-1990,* Breedon Books, 1990.

Steve Hale and Ivan Ponting, *Liverpool in Europe,* Guinness Publishing, 1992.

Ian Hargraves, *Liverpool Greats,* Sports Print Publishing in Association with *The Liverpool Echo,* 1989

Ian Hargraves, Ken Rogers and Ric George, *Liverpool: Club of the Century,* Liverpool Echo Publication, 1988.

Steve Heighway, *Liverpool: My Team,* Souvenir Press, 1977.

Brian James, *Journey to Wembley,* Marshall Cavendish, 1977.

Kevin Keegan & John Roberts, *Kevin Keegan,* Arthur Barker, 1977.

Stephen F. Kelly, *You'll never walk Alone: The Official Illustrated History of Liverpool FC,* Macdonald Queen Anne Press, 1987.

Doug Lamming, *Who's Who of Liverpool 1892-1989,* Breedon Books, 1989.

Stan Liversedge, *Liverpool 1892-1992: The Official Centenary History,* Hamlyn, 1991.

Bob Paisley, *Bob Paisley's Liverpool Scrapbook,* Souvenir Press, 1979.

Bob Paisley, *My 50 Golden Reds,* Front Page Books, 1990.

Brian Pead, *Liverpool Champions of Champions,* Breedon Books, 1990.

Brian Pead, *Liverpool a Complete Record 1892-1986,* Breedon Books, 1986.

Ivan Ponting, *Liverpool Player by Player,* Hamlyn, 1990.

Ivan Ponting and Steve Hale, *Sir Roger – the Life and Times of Roger Hunt, a Liverpool Legend,* Bluecoat Press, 1995.

Johnny Rogan, *The Football Managers,* Macdonald and Queen Anne Press, 1989.

Ken Rogers, *Everton Greats,* Sports Print Publishing in Association with *The Liverpool Echo,* 1989.

Jack Rollin, *Soccer at War, 1939-45* Willow books, Collins, 1985.

A Legend in his own time, David Glyn Associates, Chester, 1974.

Bill Shankly & John Roberts, *Shankly by Bill Shankly,* Arthur Barker, 1976.

Gerald Sinstadt & Brian Barwick, *The Great 1962-88 Derbies: Everton v Liverpool,* BBC Books, 1988.

Ian St John & Jimmy Greaves, *Football is a Funny Old Games,* Stanley Paul & Co. Ltd, 1986.

Tommy Smith, *I did it the Hard Way,* Arthur Barker, 1980.

Phil Thompson, *Do That Again Son and I'll Break Your Legs,* Virgin Books, 1996.

John Toshack, *Tosh – An Autobiography,* Arthur Barker, 1982.

Les Tiggs, David Hepton & Sid Woodhead, *Grimsby Town: A Complete Record 1878-1989,* Breedon Books, 1989.

Martin Wingfield, *So Sad, So Very Sad…The League History of Workington AFC,* Worthing Typesetting, 1992.

SPECIAL THANKS

I would like to acknowledge the support of the following bodies:

The Liverpool Daily Post and Echo Ltd
The Huddersfield Examiner
Kirklees Photographic Archive

Thanks are also due to Ken Barlow at Ebury Press for his help and assistance, and to James Howarth, Alex Cameron and Holly Bennion at Tempus.